SENTENCE-MAKING

A WRITING CRAFT WORKBOOK & MEMOIR

for Kelsey

SENTENCE-MAKING

BY

GRANT MAIERHOFER

FERAL DOVE BOOKS

BANGOR, MAINE

2024

Artists create in rebellion against the failure to create

Samuel R. Delany, Harold Bloom

INTRO-
-DUCTION

I don't personally believe much in the notion of a book on craft. The books I've read that might be called craft books only ever really interested me if the author interested me, and once elements of story-structure or POV or character choices came up I lost interest. This is not to say I was born into writing knowing exactly how I'd do what I want to do — the opposite is true. The notion of the craft book, however — the idea that I've figured it out, and am not going to share a method that breaks someone out of the cage they find themselves in as writers — is off-putting. This work, then, does not presume to be a craft book. It doesn't presume to be an anti-craft book either, but that's certainly closer to what I intended when I got started in this vein however long ago. It's a book about writing, for writers, and especially for writers interested in the sentence, and in turn for readers too. That phrasing, "interested in the sentence," already feels like the kind of thing I'd need to defend myself against for its seeming redundancy. Isn't every writer, in some form or other, interested in the sentence? Probably, sure, but I think across time, at least since the first texts began being circulated, there have been writers who engaged with language in such a way as to elucidate the wonders a sentence can hold, or pushed the sentence to its limits quite consciously. "Sentence-making," then, speaks not only to that history, but to the building realization I've had in my own work that focusing on the sentence itself can help to strip worldly concerns from the sides of what one's working on, and reach more straightforwardly into one's own gut for the thing which seem to want to be expressed — especially as opposed to those things we certainly could write, but might not scratch the same itch.

My approach is frequently autobiographical, so the book is indicative of how I've come to write the way I do, and what I tend to believe in as it regards writing. It's a bit more expressive and intuitive as opposed to academic — even as it regards the "sentence" itself; I'm not a grammarian, nor a linguist, so I approach sentences as a reader and writer the same way an art critic might treat the space of the canvas; some, certainly, can unpack types of paint, sizing distinctions, what have you, where most might address the images, their makeup, frequently needing to find their own language to do so — my tastes, in turn, tend towards works engaging with violence, extremity, or abrasiveness, both in content and in form, so I don't presume to be covering much of anything at all generally. Because of this my wording is probably somewhat crude at points, or crass, but that's only left as is because I believe honesty, being truthful in one's intent, is a vital aspect of writing, of sentence-making, and leads to the most compelling stuff — also, to be sure, I'm lazy. I've tried, throughout, to remain constantly aware of how I'd have liked to come to understand cetain things sooner than I managed to at my own pace, while also letting sentences guide me as they tend to in all of my work.

The epigraph is, as I understand it, Delany quoting an idea from Bloom. To me, it's the finest distillation of what I think of as the impulse to write, to make art, I've come across — to be sure, if you're needing more of a shot in the arm, Mary Ruefle's lectures, Nobel Prize acceptance speeches, or videos of John Cassavettes might prove more inspiring, but "artists create in rebellion against the failure to create" remains the finest because it can apply to all artists, in all circumstances. There's often a sense that one's life must prove particularly interesting and compelling for someone to be a worthwhile artist, and this has been disproven for as long as it's been perpetuated. Artists, and writers, should be concerned with the work — with form, with content; but the balance between each of these is as multitudinous and varied from writer to writer, and artist to artist, as our fingerprints. This work argues for some level of engagement with form — i.e. sentence-making — as being vital to the process of figuring out how to do this, but the content can affect the form in turn, so both are treated throughout — and of course the complicated intermingling of these factors isn't entirely a thing a person in my position can hope to transmit to someone, but probably it's worthwhile to pursue; and what's more, I don't think that's necessarily the ambition of this here work, rather, I want to consider some things, and share them, and see what's what. I think that some of the most compelling work will often come from a feeling of an inability to do anything worthwhile, and the temptation to shut oneself up and throw it all out — and perhaps the "rebellion" comes from recklessly deciding to try something out anyway, to simply try — and I think that's at the root of the quotation, the formulation. Art is a practice of opposing, of pushing back, of potential rebellion at the internal, human level — at its best — and all you've got to worry about to consider yourself an artist, a writer, is to rebel against what would otherwise be your failure to make something - whether it be something worthwhile, or something novel-shaped, or something that makes you money--that can depend from person to person, life to life--so all you've got to worry over is pushing back against the temptation to be quiet, to sit silent in the corner of living. A writer decides they're going to write, they're going to get something written down, and through that process they assume this role that's their eternal burden to pursue.

This is no rulebook, this is no set of rules. These are some thoughts that have developed over time as I've pursued writing. I'm not some philosopher. I'm not particularly sharp or well-versed in grammar, linguistics. I've tried to engage honestly with my own practice and how it's changed, and what I've learned as that's happened, and that's sort of the long and short of what's assembled here.

My only real goal is to engage with other writers who are in this process of figuring things out, to introduce some ways of looking at things that are hopefully worthwhile, and to begin a conversation with anybody who takes writing seriously, even while hopefully being unserious in your relationship to the mechanical drudgery that is inevitable. The thing I'd most hope to convey to any writer is to continue, to persist, to try very hard to realize the self that they've been tasked with figuring out. Writing can be one of the most beautiful things in the world for a person to become obsessed with — even now, working on this sentence, sitting in bed with the TV on with my wife and our dog, my living is enriched by this work — and whatever your relationship to it might be, this book hopes to affirm that.

My thought is me: that's why I can't stop. I exist because I think... and I can't stop myself from thinking. At this very moment—it's frightful—if I exist, it is because I am horrified at existing. I am the one who pulls myself from the nothingness to which I aspire.

Jean-Paul Sartre

Be Emersonian: say what no one else has the courage to say and you will be em-braced. Reveal what you would keep secret. You will stay awake when writing such a story; you will also write very, very carefully with so much at stake. Each sentence is extruded from the previous sentence; look behind you when writing, not ahead. Your obligation is to know your objects and to steadily, inexorably darken and deepen them.

Christine Schutt

THE WORLD

BEING

THAT IS

THE CASE

EVERYTHING

For a long time I've wanted to write something about sentences — the sentence—sentencing—sentence-making. I don't necessarily want to write something about sentences that treats them grammatically — I say that because, again, I'm not a grammarian. My education in these respects—respecting language, parts of speech, the word and its varied tendrils—came after my more formative educational years, as I was either ignoring lessons in my primary education, or on drugs, or hospitalized, in rehab, or doing whatever other things young people get up to from five or so years old until eighteen.

I think there were some aspects of language that appealed to me naturally, and possibly separately or possibly therein aspects of art — and perhaps it's even useful here to highlight the fact that I see these things as largely drawing from and feeding into the exact same pool, if I view "The Taking of Christ" the effect might be the same as reading from Wittgenstein or Schutt; the only important distinction anymore is I've decided, and/or been compelled to decide, that the linguistic, or sentential response, rather, that I have to either, is where I'll direct my attention — and so in the end I associate most aspects of art with aspects of language, either because of or contributing to how I turned out. I've wanted to write something that others could look to—look at—who were interested in sentences; and I've wanted most to write something that other writers could look at—look to—and feel good about their relationship to sentences — the world in its determining would most often assert that someone poring over a curious sentence for no sake beyond doing it should not feel good about it, should get on with the point; but this relishing can be an enrichment to living. I have an anxiety, I must admit, at even posturing like this, as if I have something to impart — because what in sweet hell do I know, could I even know — but I'm trying, in good faith, and sincerely, and without a sense of being better or smarter than any living being; just being merely a person merely trying to approach the notion of a sentence.

I got very interested in the idea of the sentence as this locus of attention, of expression and communication, in my early twenties; and that's continued into my thirties, where I now think of the work that I do as largely bound up by the sentence, the apparatus with which any larger works or projects are realized — so I've grown fixed in trying to write something about sentences, in these respects, something within a tradition of writers whose efforts overlap — as a point of engagement that enriches living, and enriches writing — I do not have great success, nor do I hope for it, not exactly; the thing I'm able to have any control over in this living and working is this apparatus. The Schutt quote speaks to her experience in the notorious Gordon Lish workshops, and a frequent assignment mentioned is to write something you'd never tell anybody. The result, at least in

Schutt's adaptive recreation, is a scenario wherein the writer's focus is sharpened, yet vulnerable — this fixity, then, is I guess the reward of paying one's attention thusly — the world, ideally, becoming the case at hand, then, rather than the chaotic blur of living in actuality.

These would be sentences as they regard writers, then, and as they regard readers, sure, but mostly as they regard writers—it's probably fair to think of sentences as looking at the writers, in their initial nonexistence or as they're happening, but probably how they pertain to them is more and better to the point. I say this because it took me quite some time to understand the ways in which sentences regard writers — and probably longer to even start thinking much at all of the word "sentence" or "sentences" when I wrote anything, if I'm being honest. Someone who writes poems tends to go into the thing — go into the poem — knowing the import of a line, a stanza, or at least they can learn it very quickly — words and their commingling are important to them because of the nature of poetry, the apparatus of a poem calls attention pretty naturally to the weight and sonic nature of what they're getting down. This is where your focus is rewarded in writing poetry. If you can make a line good, then you can hopefully continue to make good lines, and maybe in twenty of them you've made a good poem. Prose, though, is different — it's strange. We think of things like characters, or moods, or plots, or stories, or elements we want to include, say: murder, say: violence, say: torture, whatever content, whatever else. It can take some time, then, to bring the focus just so that it allows you to see the mechanical apparatus you happen to be working in, this being the sentence. We think about a story we want to tell, perhaps — we think about how someone spoke, or the way a room looked — but we do this first more often, and we skip the means by which we're getting any of these things accounted for, and that is the sentence— the words, arranged there — and that is the focus of this work. You can become enamored with the whole of a thing, with me that's how it started. I read books, I read about the writers of these books, and I wanted to write my own. I started too focused on the entirety of it, then. Because of this, the pieces comprising that whole were like boring little scraps of aluminum. I couldn't figure it out. Slowly, with much effort, I got fixated closer and closer, which has made the work live.

Let's start, then, with an example.

I pulled off my gloves and dug my fingers into the earth, met with worm — moved aside — and removed clods to make a bed.

I've rewritten a version of this sentence many times over the past few years. It started with a loner character taking his coveralls off in the park after work and commingling with the ground. Then it was an angry person, trying to punch a hole into the world. Now it's this. So what can we make of this. It could be picked apart in linguistic terms, noun-phrases, verb-phrases — the former, i.e. "the young man," usually ties to the latter, i.e. "killed a boar," making the subject-predicate of a typical sentence; or grammatical ones, ensuring subject-verb agreement are coherent, that elements are well-placed or something like a comma splice or split infinitive needn't be revised.

These are elements which might be enjoyable or useful for a writer or reader or another human person to direct towards a sentence like this. I've enjoyed and found use in such a thing. For our purposes, though, and this overall endeavor of "sentence-making," I want to look at this sentence as a thing put there by a human, for some apparent reason or under some apparent compulsion, and see what it might offer the writer of such a sentence, or its reader.

We begin with the fragment "I pulled off my gloves and dug," which feels a bit like a line from a country song, and even follows the rhythm of something like "slide off of your satin sheets," or "I shot a man in Reno, just…" Or if not these musical referents then at least the child-like rhythm of da-dum da-dum da-dum.

11

From my own perspective, as a person who felt compelled to write such a sentence, I liked the idea that this figure was shedding some version of himself before doing something sort of naturalistic and vile. If he's digging his grave, it might even make more sense for the gloves to stay on, but the sentence, and presumably the piece, opens with their removal.

"I pulled off my gloves and dug my fingers into the earth". Probably it's just pushing the line of needing some kind of breaking point, a comma or dash or semicolon. Speaking it out loud there's a small sense of exasperation by the end, but it's not too bad. The image appeals to me I think because the movements seem like mirrored images of the other, taking off, i.e. sort of cleansing an object of something, or ridding it, only to then surround it in dirt, soil, earth. A freedom is followed immediately by another kind of encasement. Not hands, either, as digging one's hands into the earth treats them as mitts, whole entities. I think during days working, or running errands, or even simply days spent sitting around not doing anything at all, a sentence like this can get into your head as a kind of linguistic anti-jingle, bubbled up from the un- or subconscious thinking as a rejoinder to the nothingness of being—more exactly probably the somethingness.

"met with worm—moved aside — and removed clods to make a bed," I'm interested in serpentinous moves a sentence can make like this. Robert Kloss is doing brilliant things with en- or em-dashes, lines which break up thinking, disrupt moments, events — Laurence Sterne, too, did this brilliantly. The fingers meet with a worm, the protection of the gloves is gone, the fingers now meet something slimy there, which is then moved aside. I tend to agree with Cormac McCarthy's idea that punctuation and the sort of nonessential dressings that can overwhelm a page are probably best left off, but the dash applied in such a way remains an important thing to me, like a way of digging into the contours of a sentence — or taking a breather — before returning to whatever's at hand.

This notion of the clod, or even sod, is something I've long been enamored with. I wrote a story once called "Watertown Bodily" wherein I wrote "of a sudden his finger pawed the sod," or something thereabouts. The same way that sentences like this will often present themselves up from your mind, particular words and phrasings and even just sounds, portions of words, will persist, and should be followed in this process of sentence-making. Jean Cocteau advised listening to your critics and what they point out as particularly negative in your work, or simply bad, and to cultivate that, for it is you. Trusting the language that stays with you is similar. I've been randomly saying the name "John Grisham" as a stand-in for just about every possible kind of word for a long time, because there's something in it that feels right to me. A phrase like "removed clods to make a bed" is the result of that kind of internal trust and acceptance of the linguistic sounds that resonate with me.

Whether it's a "good" or a "bad" sentence, or a correct or grammatically-sound sentence, seems to me besides the point of the kind of writing I'm interested in looking at here. I'm concerned less with the after of writing, the analysis, and more with how we get through these first steps, and how we learn to attune ourselves to the voice within us that will most reliably generate work that's satisfying for us. Whether you're writing genre fiction, screenplays, or poems, this thinking seems to be the most logical for a writer for it's the kind of thinking which will align with work you're most naturally inclined to make.

A sentence is a sort of commitment the writer makes, only so that they're then able to carry out the remainder of whatever it is they find themselves needing to write. I've heard of writers of fiction who might be prompted, or asked by friends, why they don't write a memoir, an autobiography; or conversely, writers of memoir who might be asked if they've ever had an idea they've wanted to try in the purely fictional realm. My inclination is these writers are only asked this kind of thing because their work, through its determined interior voice, seems so particular, so distinct, and thus an interviewer, or friend, might feel compelled to wonder at what else that perspective might generate. I've heard, just as often, of these writers of fiction saying something on the order of "I already have, the work I've done is me," or if they're a memoirist they might explain they've done their imagining right there, they've already pushed the idea in the work as much as they've felt they needed to. Of course this can't be seen as a universal truth, but there is truth within it as a kind of parable for the writer. When you trust your internal sense of your language, and you figure out how to best enact that sense in your work, the whole of you is brought to the process. David Foster Wallace talked about the divide between two academic fields he considered pursuing long term in undergrad. He said philosophy, which he'd excelled at, and which his father made his life exploring, used — I'm paraphrasing — maybe sixty per cent of his thinking; whereas fiction, the field he inevitably pursued, used closer to ninety. Part of this, I think it's fair to hazard — and Wallace as a writer is as guided by language as any we're likely to find — has to do with the ability a writer in a more expressive realm has to engage the language within their own skull.

You have to begin, and you have to begin in such a way that you're not entirely holding on. Something is guiding you, something else is guiding you, and in the process of enacting this something in language you're then pushing yourself to a small problem, the only solution to which is to finish writing this sentence, and these sentences in turn, in the order your transcription would appear to dictate. Learning to hold onto these bits of language as they present themselves can often mean the writing of an entirely new project — holding onto the phrases that stick to you, or place names that feel evocative, or the names of pets or individuals that echo in your brain more than others. For me, it's bits of phrasing like the previous example, and they'll change in the process of my recalling them, and I'll carry them with me, hoping that someday I'll get to put them down as rightly as I'm able. Becoming attuned to one's interior language is as important as registering the mastery of others at their craft, and often more important, and more generative. Devoting time to listening to yourself seriously, as this can guide you not only to compelling work for others to read, but satisfying work for you as the maker. Nicholson Baker talked once about the work he needed to do to get his book The Anthologist written. He'd sit in a chair with a camera facing him, and he would talk about everything he felt he knew about poetry. The book winds up taking the form of a sidestepped introduction to an anthology of poems, but the language to get the thing started didn't present itself fully until he sat down and just started talking. Mary Robison, too, when she wrote *Why Did I Ever*, would drive around with a recording device, dictating observations and thoughts to herself, and would then write these and transcribe these onto index cards on a portable typewriter. Frederick Barthelme, a master of the deeply intuited sentence, has dictated multiple books, and the result has consistently been charged in a way at once characteristic of the author, while feeling oddly new. Countless stories exist too of Joyce dictating *Finnegans Wake* at the end of his life — the infamous episode where someone knocked at the door, his amanuensis said "come in," and Joyce said to leave it in the book — but the immediacy of John Fante's dictation of *Dreams From Bunker Hill* to his wife at the end of his life might serve us even better. Blinded and in and out of hospitals from diabetes, Fante wrote one more book, narrating it to his wife, and returning to the things he'd written and agonized over for that marrow-deep humanity he's now revered for, and the result is arguably one of his greatest accomplishments. The language does exist within, and these are steps one can take to finding it, and mining it for its inherent worth.

When I set out to write a sentence, I'm shutting off certain parts of my brain, intentionally, while cranking really high the parts of my brain that contribute to the physical act of writing something down — I don't mean on paper, necessarily, because I think it makes sense to think of writing as something that's physically done (Capote's "that's not writing, it's typing" re: Jack Kerouac made me more curious to read Kerouac; and I remain unsentimental about apparatuses with which one writes, though lately I do love pens) with the body, whether you're narrating via machinery a la Hob Broun — a sentence-maker par excellence whose work is worth your exploring (1) — or with one pencil, recurring, recurring, a la Peter Markus.

There's an arcade in the town next to mine that I like to visit with my wife and children sometimes. There's a game there that I'm guessing most people have tried a version of. It's essentially a large wheel. You pull down on this stocky metal lever and the wheel spins, eventually arriving at a number which corresponds to the number of tickets you'll receive for that spin. One day I found myself really hitting it on that machine. In that build up I got excited, and I tried to simply, physically, repeat my pulls on the lever, until high numbers were reached again. I don't know why this happens, exactly, but I started to get bad spins when focused like that. What I needed to do was let my mind sort of hover there a moment, noncommittal, but open to the world, and then push with my hands sort of removed from me, physical, but separate from my thinking self.

(1) This opening to Broun's story, "Ice Water," which was recently reissued on Kindle by Open Road Media, in his collection Cardinal Numbers, amply demonstrates his control of the sentence-everything, even the name, Schenck, feels evocative, drenched in the person who wrote it:

Even in mid-December, wearing two sweaters, window glass rattling in dead putty there at the back of the shop, Schenck drank only ice water. It rippled on his throat, against the wall of his stomach. It cleared his palate and cleansed his bladder. He drank down a gallon or more in a day, not from an excess of thirst-his appetites were diffident-but vigilantly, to maintain a pattern of comfort and good feeling. Always, Schenck had guarded his habits.

With a spin or two I found I got the jackpot, something that's never happened to
me in a situation like that — I consider
myself unlucky, or pretty unlucky, really, at least as it regards this kind of
thing. Now, whether this practice did in
fact directly correspond with me getting
the jackpot is — at least largely — imma-
terial. It did, but those machines are so
finicky that to assign causation is tricky,
or meaningless. What mattered was I did it.
I entered that state, vaguely meditative
but present, doing something but not task-
ing myself with really doing something.

Probably this sounds tenuous, or something;
or unreliable, but it's close to what I'm
saying, and what I'm advocating in such
an effort. Possibly one of the frustrating
things a writer deals with is the sense that
technical ability is best served by a kind
of feeling, a will, or a willing towards
a lack thereof; but technical ability on
its own seems to best serve the after of
writing, the finishing touches — not editing, not revising, as these are very much
the before, during, *present* of writing.

You position yourself to get something
written, and you open your mind to language, and you put something down, and you
find that this something calls for something else, and so on, until you're comfortable putting a period on the whole
mess. Kay Redfield Jamison highlights the
ways in which a manic-depressive temperament might be conducive to art-marking —
or at least analogous to it—that you need

the manic state to get something down, to get something out, a recklessness even; and then the depressive state that follows makes your critique of the work that much more biting, so that in this procession a work is created, and refined, and readied for the world to engage with. I agree with Jamison in lots of ways, but I think the benefits from this kind of practice highlight something else in turn. To get a draft written, it helps to be a little dumb, at least as it regards the creation of the thing. If you're not trying to be smart, and you're letting yourself, sort of dumbly, enter into the process of the thing, the not knowing of the thing, to push it somewhere without thinking too much about it, you're rewarded not only with word count, but with work that genuinely surprises you. Though he's fallen out of favor, Kenneth Goldsmith's writing on dumb-smart, dumb-dumb, smart-smart, and smart-dumb writers and artists distills what I'm talking about nicely: I am dumb. Dumb is an ill-prepared slacker, riding on hunches and intuition. This aspect, this intuition, gets at what I'm talking about. As writers we're told countless exterior things to get things done, but sitting down, that internal sense, that intuition, can be trusted. Even if it takes eighty revisions, the more reckless and dumb you sit down prepared to be, the more likely it is you'll write something as unique as Broun's opening. Plus, it's far easier to revise something seemingly crazed than it is something you overthink and render sort of safe, or inert, in the process — trust me, I've edited my bad manuscripts, and abandoned as many as my sense of the thing would allow me, and opening a draft and having no idea what I was attempting is far better than opening something I can't bear to retread.

Of course there are writers who are engaged on every level and utilizing their smarts to get something finished—Robert Sapolsky certainly seems like one, and David Foster Wallace too, and in turn Zadie Smith seems to be one a majority of the time — but at some point trusting in that intuition, the internal voice that seems to speak out when we listen to it—when we allow ourselves to listen to it—helps us to develop a relationship with our own inner language, and it's that language that will give newness to the work we're trying to accomplish. This is the kind of thing that allows a writer like Jeffrey DeShell to engage with Herman Melville's Pierre, or, the Ambiguities, but to do so in a way that feels entirely new, or novel; or for DeShell too to engage directly with actual films and actual filmmakers in Arthouse, but doing so intuitively—processing through his perspective, his lens, his gut — and opening new doors for the writing he's doing by following where the source text takes him. Plenty of writers, too, talk about transcribing the pages of other writers, and it's a highly educational thing, but not enough is said about that glorious moment when you're transcribing — it might be the intentional transcription of Hemingway by Bret Easton Ellis and Hunter S. Thompson;

it might be transcription for incorporation of longer quotes from a novel for a review — and you start to intuit something different, somehow you're guided, you've been led, and your own mind and your own voice begins to take over, and suddenly you no longer need the source text at all.

Writing, in certain respects, is a practice of creating problems for yourself, then developing solutions to those problems. Writers often mistake this to mean—as do all forms of artists, inevitably, inevitably — that they should explode their entire life to get some interesting work, but you can amply generate a lifetime of problems for yourself in the work and the work alone, which you're not tasked with solving — the strange case of Thomas Wolfe seems ample evidence of this. You're opening the lines of communication, then, and letting them be open, remain open. If you sit down knowing every single thing you want to get down, you'll find you run out of things to say rather quickly. If you allow yourself — again, allow, these are permissions we must give ourselves — to dwell a bit in the uncertain act of putting language to ideas, to thoughts, to scenes, to anything written, you'll find you'll be rewarded for that openness; given means to get the thing written in the particular fashion it begs to be written.

Back, once more, alas, to the clods of earth:

I pulled off my gloves and dug my fingers into the earth, met with worm — moved aside — and removed clods to make a bed.

Qualification in writing is often a sort of tepid endeavor. You want to avoid it. It's associated with the passive voice, but that's in turn a kind of unuseful reduction. It's associated with making excuses, with dancing around something. This might be valid, but it also ignores a great—perhaps the greatest — strain in the history of writing. It precedes writing, actually — in speech. The recordings of speech and the repetitions of speech. So even though this is an ambling sentence, perhaps occasionally a qualifying sentence, it could be uplifted by this for its proximity to the spoken, the gut-level speech. We might know the outcome of the Peloponnesian War. We might know brass tacks. X won, Y lost, halved, the remaining went home. This wasn't the endeavor, then, not really, not solely on its own, when the thing got written down, after it got talked about for however many years by however many people who neglected to write it down. We've wanted people who waffled, who could linger over things, first in speech and then thusly in writing, we wanted to follow their thinking, to understand their perspective. Like dance, dance in its proper form, the sort of dancing a writer, or a speaker might do can be as equally compelling as the digestible bits someone might take away from a face-based piece of reporting — I am a person who worships Wikipedia, the whole endeavor, but when I try (and I do try) to read something on Wikipedia, I find that I need to move around to make any sense of it, to make my own sense of it, because reading straight through is not dissimilar from reading just the facts, and the fact is we process information in a lingering, meandering way, so the best sentence-makers do some of this ahead of time, and we follow them.

That sentence, then, with its meanderings. You can see the pullings on the thing itself — the breakages, the attempts at something bigger than Jack and Jill went up the hill— and see where they've led to this unique bit of momentary language. Even if it's all you know, all you take from a thing written, it might just be enough. It ought to be enough. And although I feel tempted to make an apology for sharing a sentence of my own preoccupation coming right out at the first of this book I'm equally mollified by the reality that this thing is not the thing—or the kind of thing—I'm really worried about. The description is not the thing I'm worried about, or what's described in such a sentence, and thus it's a good point to leave off on this first sort of trial, that the thing described cannot be, or will not be, in this particular case, nearly as important as the language with which it's described, being hopefully a kind of modeling of my own personal attunement to my own internal language.

I think now the sensible thing is to look at some sentences from elsewhere, sentences that I did not write, to try and ascertain just what makes them seem to tick, and to return these examples to the task at hand of approaching writing not as something bound by rules and orders, but as something bound up in the human spirit, a register that we can look for and find through the process of composition.

So then the order is that a white way of being round is something suggesting a pin and is it disappointing, it is not, it is so rudimentary to be analysed and see a fine substance strangely, it is so earnest to have a green point not to red but to point again.

This is the kind of sentence you can take a bath in. This is a sauna of a sentence, a warm embrace of a thing. If I'm to be entirely honest, when I'm looking at this sentence I don't want to start at the beginning in my mulling over its qualities. For whatever reason it's that "it is not" that grabs my attention firstly. We have this sort of preamble, this physical description of something that's vaguely mathematical but vague too in that this vaguely mathematical thing is disappointing — to whom, and just why? And the lead into it: "and is it disappointing" (of course it is, it all is, or no, it isn't, it isn't — but is the round pin thing a button?) "it is not," so is this a question and answer to the disappointing component? I'm not entirely sure. I'm quite sure that I don't need to be entirely sure. You can't open a sentence this much and expect your reader to close it. You don't scream at someone for twenty minutes about your job anxiety and then ask them if it's time for a career move. A sentence like this isn't written to be neatly tucked away. So we're used to the set up it is… is it not? and here we have its sort of opposite, but even then it's just slippery enough to elude being a mere opposite to that construction. Possibly too there's something to be extracted from Stein's sort of manifesto on writing "Composition as Explanation," first given as a talk and then published by Leonard and Virginia Woolf's Hogarth Press(3). In some ways as elusive as anything she ever published, "Composition as

(3) Available via Poetry Foundation here: https://www.poetryfoundation.org/articles/69481/composition-as-explanation, for a sampling, that might as well be applied to Tender Buttons as all of Stein: The composition is the thing seen by every one living in the living they are doing, they are the composing of the composition that at the time they are living in the composition of the time in which they are living. It is that that makes living a thing they are doing. Nothing else is different, of that almost any one can be certain. The time when and the time of and the time in that composition is the natural phenomena of that composition and of that perhaps every one can be certain.

Explanation" tries nevertheless to pin down Stein's approach to sentence-making as it bears on her own practice: "Everything is the same except composition and as the composition is different and always going to be different everything is not the same." Stein is talking about—and she points to all art throughout—the interventional nature of art-making, of writing, of composition, and she picks apart this idea by pointing to differences and samenesses, by discussing time within the context of a work and time outside of the work. It's dense, recursive stuff, from a dense, recursive writer, but there is something fundamental to draw from it for writers: your work should embrace its difference, as its difference is its one truly sustaining thing, its one truly irreplaceable thing. She advocates a sort of constant awareness of the thing at hand, and this in-the-moment writing explains how she might've arrived at a sentence like the one included here. There's a movement to it, wherein whatever's just been said is being left behind in the name of utilizing this process of composition and embracing a lack of similarity; a pursuit of difference. In fact, trying to make this the operative mode of the whole ordeal, moving away from similarity to the artifice at hand, and pressing on it until the same sentence can be reversed awkwardly upon itself just like the opening and closing constructions "is it disappointing/it is not."

Returning, then, to the beginning, "So then the order is that a white way of being round," and I assure you the movement from which this is plucked offers little in terms of comprehension of the meaning or message or signified of what's being enacted here, and possibly this is for the better — Stein, perhaps more than Joyce, could relish apparent nonsense because there seemed always to be a playfulness in the work; on the one hand we can get mad and think, ach, this is garbage, nonsense, on the other, we can bathe in the game. Stein's writing, and especially Stein's writing in Tender Buttons, from which this is excerpted, is a sort of pure writing, a linguistic act that doesn't necessarily call for any referent, and can simply exist as it likes to, there upon the floor, or in your lap, with no more logical underpinning than a cat sprawling on the rug throughout the day, occasionally stretching itself and yawning, digging its claws into the fabric. Per Rothko, the subject of the writing is the writing, not necessarily the written, or the book, or the poem, or the story, the writing. "[A] white way of being round is something suggesting a pin and is it disappointing, it is not, it is so rudimentary to be analysed and see a fine substance strangely, it is so earnest to have a green point not to red but to point again." This sort of thing, often I think it proves frustrating to people — and certainly I've been plenty frustrated reading this kind of writing — or for people, because the assumption is she's only kind of clacking away on a typewriter or with her pencil and seeking no stable entity for the work, trying to tell no story, not even really offering us a poem consisting entirely of language because we have so many of the little dull bits of sentences that kind of make us frustrated, mad, like any child might be able to do this sort of thing, and thus it can't possibly be taken at its face value, or is better not taken at all. Stein's adherence to a kind of Cubist writing can help a bit, as can situating her in her milieu, but asserting that one way of reading takes primacy over any other is part of the trouble Stein was working against in writing in such a way — if we can accept a painter being fed up with recreation only, can we accept a writer being fed up with the impositions put on us since writing came to be? Contrarily, though, for the reader, and too for the writer, why would we compel ourselves to read something that so departs in so many important ways from what we've been led to believe reading, and writing, should be? What's at work here?

This is a tough thing to express, to argue, but an important point to argue in the broader practice of sentence-making. Stein sat down, and worked on things — physically, physically — and tried to put the whole of being into what she tried to write down, and she was removed at least by one distance in the sense that her expression was more important than what was actually expressed. So not unlike a lecturer grunting, making jokes besides, rambling on in tangents, trying to find their way to wherever it is they once were, or wanted to go, Stein writes a sentence that contains materials we're used to having read in other people's sentences, but we're left with the physical matter there and made to figure out on our own just what in the hell is the use of such a thing. The materials are similar, but strangely distributed. The contours of the sentence in English prose are there, but atypically, askew. Like every other thing, the sentence is an apparatus with which a person can aspire to achieve some sort of desired effect. The less knowledge there is about this desired effect, the better for you and the better for whomsoever should enter and encounter your sentence, so as to let the situation be as open and welcoming to the human spirit as possible — because desired effects are not mirrors, and our readers will not simply intuit our desires from the work and follow in lockstep.

Often these two things are at odds, a writer and a reader. You write something because of the point you're trying to make, either concrete and argumentative, or abstract and bound up in the act of writing itself. Your reader reads the same thing because they're hoping to tap into some mood, some aspect or aspects of being, or some sort of truth about the state of the human spirit. It gets tangled, is what I'm saying. Intent, result, these things confusedly entwine with one another from the first draft of composing to your very last reader's last moment with the text. In Stein, especially, where there was this sense of something happening in writing, and in art, and there were conversations she was having about this stuff, and thus very self-consciously she was trying to enact something different. Intent on both sides can and does blur the messaging, so it's important sometimes — and with certain approaches especially, here, namely, Modernism — to let the messaging fall secondary to the sort of presence you're hoping to occupy as the writer of this kind of thing, this sentence. It's why, I think, my reaction initially was a desire to take a bath in the sentence, to let it wash over me. Partly it's because I haven't read every single text on or about Stein and her entire milieu, partly it's because it's such a curious approach to a sentence that the best way in to me seems to be an atmospheric one.

Nicholson Baker once said that poetry is slow-motion prose. Whether this is in the utmost true, it does convey something about sentence-making that often doesn't register for people who find themselves making sentences: it is on the same plane as, and of a piece with, poetry, the line, the stanza. Stein is a writer who somehow manages slow-slow-motion prose, where a lineatedness might actually relieve some of those readers disinclined to bathe in *Tender Buttons*. Sentences are an apparatus the writer has at their disposal, and thus should be treated as seriously as the poet treats the line, treats the contained space wherein they've got their shot at conveying some humanity, or otherwise. Whether a sentence, in turn, is sped-up, in Baker's estimation, is not for me to say — or not necessarily my feeling, to put it clearer — but the process ought to be treated as reverentially as some divinely tetched poet taking dictation in an opium den in 1880s Paris, a bullet still lodged in their wrist from a disgruntled lover. As a writer of sentences you are taking dictation from something burrowed in your guts, and learning to access that — to open yourself up to that — is half the battle of taking sentence-making seriously, and treating your writing with the reverence it does deserve.

Thinking in these terms, then, it seems
useful to rearrange the sentence to
see what all might be making it tick.

*So then the order is that a white
way of being round is something
suggesting a pin and is it disappointing,
it is not, it is so rudimentary
to be analysed and see a fine substance strangely,
it is so earnest to have a green point not to red but to point
again.*

It's more palatable in this formation, I think — I know it could be better broken up, but I don't want to reinvent it any more than I have here. I think the long sentence — especially the long sentence that utilizes a good bit of, I don't want to say filler, but let's say packaging — is immediately daunting for a reader, while conversely being exhilarating and natural for a writer. The long-sentence writer is the rambling person writer. There's something here that I think needs parsing. Loud, relentless guitar music can be infinitely entertaining and compelling for the performer, but it's less likely to maintain the attention of a listener than something more digestible — there are exceptions, of course, and there are performers who can prove so compelling as to welcome in the audience to their performances (Bill Orcutt can do this, Albert Ayler could do this, Keiji Haino can certainly do this), but by and large there are types of music that undeniably appeal far more to the performer than the audience. I think reading and writing can often be quite similar. If we see a brick of text on a page, for instance, and it's unbroken, depending on the context we'll feel some kind of way about it. If we've gone from the speedy fragments of Adler's Speedboat to a monotonous digression from Pierre; or, the Ambiguities misprinted into the text, we'll feel some kind of way about it. In Proust, sure, that's par for the course, and part of the endeavor, so it's not too surprising.

Proust, in this regard, might be close to Glenn Gould, or Scott Ross, someone who manages to be both performer-satisfying and audience-satisfying, through manner, through textual tradition. In the work, though, of a linguistically-dense writer like, say, Christine Schutt, or Garielle Lutz, the sentences themselves are so immense and evocative that shorter bursts of paragraphs, and even broken-off sentences seem to fit the experience, to follow the mood of the writer and the reader both. If, on the other hand, we're reading something about how to replace a sink, long, billowy sentences would prove frustrating, as they might in turn in a spy thriller, a Twitter thread, a text, or other spaces in which a sentence has a function that precludes, or elides, meditative, expanded sentencing.

Stein, I think, probably occupies both the writer-centric and potentially the reader-centric here. Especially within *Tender Buttons*, where shorter, arguably funner, bursts are the rule, but the wording and the syntax is so incredibly dense and expressive that even one sentence — this sentence — can feel simultaneously daunting and gleeful, overwhelming and subconscious. If you're not so generous as to view that sentence as gleeful, open up *The Making of Americans*, where daunting is the rule, and glee only comes after you've beaten your head through your boss's wall in that office building of a novel — it's great, it's wonderful.

The stanza-fication model does seem to help. The stanzafication. "So then the order is that a white/way of being round is something/suggesting a pin and is it disappointing,/it is not, it is so rudimentary/to be analysed and see a fine substance strangely,/it is so earnest to have a green point not to red but to point again." So we can now picture an item, possibly a little pin–button, tender button — with a white portion on the top where perhaps you'd push the button, and possibly the actual point is painted green? There may be a redness too? It's so rudimentary to be analysed, so is it rudimentary to be the object of analysis? Or is this item so simple as to transcend analysis, or make it rudimentary to do it? Or is this entire sentence made of such rudimentary materials as to preclude analysis?

To be analysed and see a fine substance strangely — I like that. Intaking something simple and seeing it strangely, a fine — either fine as in sand, or fine as in OK — and rendering it strangely, or it being strange, or being rendered strangely, seeing it, this substance, this matter, through a glass darkly. And can we even infer at all, ever, about whether Stein would care to be looked at in this way, and would it even matter? She wrote the thing. She put it out into the world in this state, this recursive state. She took her shit. So it would seem at the least she'd allow us was this, would be this sort of picking apart, this recursive reading. It's a sentence sort of containing six different lines, of thought or poetic sequencing, and all together they don't necessarily point to any one thing, but refer back to the lingual, the lingual act of writing, of saying, the saying of the thing in such a way as to embrace possibly its musicality — though there are far more apparently musical moments in *Tender Buttons*, so perhaps what's being explored really, embraced, rather, is its vagueness, a testament to how the saying of the thing can only lead you further from the thing at hand, the case — the thing in saying, in saying being different, the thing different, the different thing. The world being everything that is, that is the case — we don't have here a world, or a case, and we've got to reckon with the existence of the sentence nevertheless, the sentence in its oddity, the sentence in its colorless green ideas sleep furiously oddity. It's frustrating, but there are avenues in, ways of cutting it to its pieces. Even if the avenues are fogged over, perhaps Stein felt or liked the fog — who doesn't like fog? And perhaps the street signs have eroded with time, the saying of the thing can sometimes prove to be enough, so we should let her say it.

So then the order is that a white way of being round is something suggesting a pin and is it disappointing, it is not, it is so rudimentary to be analysed and see a fine substance strangely, it is so earnest to have a green point not to red but to point again.

Try retyping it yourself. Or better still, write it out by hand. Take this, a strange sentence that can only be strange, and only asks to live in its oddity, and just rewrite it, or retype it, and see. She's giving us permission, as readers, as writers, to have thoughts that do not adhere, or conform, perhaps even to her own sense of anything at all. A gift, a nauseating strange little gift. It's there.

So then the order is that a white way of being round is something suggesting a pin and is it disappointing, it is not, it is so rudimentary to be analysed and see a fine substance strangely, it is so earnest to have a green point not to red but to point again.

There's a moment in Salman Rushdie's memoir *Joseph Anton* where he's engaging with an audience at an Italian book festival, and someone is wondering whether political positions, or ideological motives, were necessary in literature. Someone, either Rushdie or one of the Italians, says that literature is about sentences. At first glance this seems like potentially a bit of a reduction, or a reductive way of looking at literature, at writing, but when you learn to sort of open yourself up to this as the ideal locus of your attention as a writer, as a person who attempts to enact literature, it becomes clear how true it really is. Yes, writers can and should tell stories, and yes, they can wage arguments, and yes, they can attempt to encapsulate experience; and yes each of these things can suffice as motive when you sit down and try to figure out how it is you're going to say whatever it is you think you might like to say. However, learning to think of the sentence as first and foremost the thing deserving of your attention, you're then capable of accessing a level of communication that eludes mere communication, and can transcend to a level that might be seen as mystical—or spiritual, in the bare sense of the human spirit, the spirit of human being. Often, the notion of prose, of sentences, is seen as a mechanical concern, a grammatical thing, a derision when compared with the big stuff, the real apparent heart of writing. Poetry, by comparison, is seen as shot through with the romantic, with being expressive, with language in its pure sense, and what I've come to realize is that prose writers from Donald E. Westlake to Marguerite Young have tapped into the pure energy of the language but in sentences. Instead of being the means to the end of the essay, the novel, the story, the sentences of any particular work can be ends in themselves. What's more, although the likes of Henry James or Edmund Wilson might've indicated there is this heightened, artful prose, and the rest exists in a state of poppy inferiority, the reality is I stop myself in awe of the sentences of Westlake as I do Young, Proust, Thomas Harris, and the list only grows. Contrary to certain schools of thought, there is a way in which this focus on sentences doesn't only lead to Faulkner, or Melville. Obviously these are fine destinations, but in my experience opening myself up to language can enhance even non-literary experiences. Snatches of dialogue in film can resonate all the more, and I'll carry them with me the same as that previous sentence, because I'm invested in language, via the sentence, and not merely invested in a certain strata of literature.

The case, the case of things, the world's case — it all seems to be far more complicated than we've been interested in realizing, or acknowledging, and this work is being written as much as a way of thinking about writing as it is a testament to the incredible enchantments of prose, of sentences. Where they've often been thought of as largely mechanical things en route to some sort of bigger apparatus in writing, an openness to their energy frequently helps these bigger apparatuses to feel less daunting, which is a problem I run into constantly as a writer, a professor, a reader, and a friend of other readers who might not want to bother with Proust, or even Knausgaard. If I think comparatively about albums, even from bands I love dearly, there are inevitably songs on their releases I skip over, sometimes almost violently. Does that mean my relationship to pieces of that entire project don't matter at all? Why couldn't sections, sentences, distillations of language in these larger apparatuses, function similarly?

Possibly another good analog would be the materials that go into the painting of visual artworks. Beginning with vague tints achieved through mixing berries and the like before someone underwent the painting of a bull on the wall of a cave, the materials for visual artwork have doubtless improved, but they consist of certain fundamentals still. Color, white, black, and the perspective of the person looking at it, rendering something, making choices about size, et cetera. Similarly, writers have used a set of materials that have changed in terms of speed, accessibility, and aspects of design, while the communicative process, speech, and emphasis, have remained relatively static. The results — at the ambitions — of these dynamics, and materials, though, have experienced drastic shifts — the work of Pollock seems huge here; the same tools, but employed in a way that broke the sound barrier for visual art — the sprawling approach to sentence-making in a work like Moby-Dick, or the intuitive and relentlessly referential approach in James Joyce's later work parallel Pollock nicely — still sentences, still language on a page, but so much more. The basic tools advance only slightly — and frankly they don't seem to need to — yet even then writers and painters are still called upon to use these things to enact something drawing from the same original well, a person, reacting to something, makes something else. Often, contemporary writers and artists romanticize slightly older forms of writing or visualizing something and make their presence known by relying on antiquated material to process our contemporary world. The converse happens too, with writers like Darby Larson feeding language through computer software to generate something else. Inevitably we do return to those fundamental elements, however, and it's my experience that the sooner we arrive at that, the more effective our work is likely to be, not just for a reader, but perhaps most importantly for ourselves.

Sentence-making, then, can look like Pollock, and certainly it does in Burroughs, in Schutt, in Jason Schwartz. It can also look drastically simple, like Rothko's images of blocks of color, in the work of say Bobbie Ann Mason, Frederick Barthelme, Amy Hempel, Zachary German or even Diane Williams in a sense. And then too the comparative framework of music is helpful.

Stripped down to its simplest elements, music is sound and silence—sound and not-sound, to go further. Painting is presence of paint and non-presence of paint. Writing is word and not-word, or no-word. Embracing this model, and not overwhelming oneself with trying to vomit forth an entire work, conceived in the mind and carefully worked over until it transcribes wholesale—apparently Rachel Cusk does this, I've never managed it — makes the process of writing not only more intuitive and rewarding, but more likely to remain open to the possibilities that haven't yet been tapped. That is often where the art of any one writer really lives, in saying the thing in the way only they can. This inner thing, this voice, this khora, to use Gordon Lish's phrasing from Kristeva, can prove limitless once it begins to be called upon, and in the ensuing pages we'll try and figure out avenues that can help us in finding, visiting, and revisiting that pool of language held in the skull of every living being. If this seems like a quasi-spiritual endeavor, something to do with more than the authoring of novels, or stories, or essays, that's because in my experience that's what it's had to be. I came to writing because of a great shift in my existence, and a need to process that in a manner I could stomach, where I wasn't simply vomiting it up in a therapist's office — though I've done that too. It is a human endeavor, this sense of sentence-making, and my belief in art takes on a religious dimension because it's through this

I've taken in a fuller sense of being and the universe, and I treat it accordingly.

To continue the conversation about the form sentences might take, and what we might glean from these forms when trying to generate our own work, the use of examples seems the most effective tool, or resource. When teaching, although it can feel sort of old-fashioned, nothing makes me feel better than to have the sentences of someone else projected next to me, trying to unpack them, as I do think this kind of work not only unpacks how such things are accomplished, it helps both myself and my students to prioritize language in our lives, something which, to put it slightly dramatically, feels terribly vital, while being perhaps at least slightly under siege. The notion of an opening sentence, in particular, would appear to try for more than a sentence situated in the middle of some humdrum paragraph about a rainy morning. To refer again to Lish's various coinages, for him the opening sentence is the attack sentence, which seems useful at least to begin a discussion of the types of sentences we aspire to distribute throughout our works (4). As previously stated, I think of writing as a process of causing problems for oneself — in the work and possibly outside of the work, though long stretches of my life have gotten muddled in the latter and I've done far more with the former in terms of actual writing written—and finding ways to solve those problems. Similar to an attack, though conceived of

(4) A note re: Gordon Lish. My understanding of what a sentence could really do is frequently informed by his ideas, though I've never been able to take a class with him, and my sense is carved from readings and rereadings more than anything else. I do think he's probably the great genius of sentences—alongside maybe Stanley Fish, though Lish is far more useful for writers—and employ his ideas with sincere reverence for all he's done for the practice of writing. If you're interested in finding distillations or demonstrations of his ideas, I'd highly recommend Sam Lipsyte's first collection, Venus Drive, as well as Garielle Lutz's Partial List of People to Bleach, which contains an introduction from Lish and Lutz's indispensable essay "The Sentence is a Lonely Place", as well as Conversations with Gordon Lish, Lish's Collected Fictions—for my money the greatest resource a writer could ever happen upon—as well as Jason Schwartz's A German Picturesque, all of Christine Schutt's work, and any issue of The Quarterly you're able to get your hands on, as well as probably hundreds of other things.

slightly differently, your opening sentence should be a commitment, a promise, of something that's going to follow after, something you're ideally not entirely certain of when you write such a sentence. It's opening, beginning, a communication, and opening yourself to this exchange, which you'll then encounter sentence-by-sentence until you feel you've finished the thing. Seeing it as an exchange, rather than say a speech, or a lecture, as your own encounter with this language as much as your someday reader's, matters here a great deal, as it starts to let you see your work as a thing eventually readable, printable, transmittable, and it makes the editing process there from the outset, and not some sneaky horrid thing you've got to confront half closing your eyes. I remark on this elsewhere, but the longer I write the more that I find that little fragments of opening sentences or closing ones will present themselves, and often the best means of utilizing these is to let them marinate, rather than scribble down every possible thing, because the longer you're able to do so, the more that sentence is likely to lead to another sentence — to in effect need another sentence — and still others, until the thing takes shape, ideally powered entirely by its singular phrasing.

There is a wide range as to how an opening sentence can, or should, look, could sound, but I want to engage with several particularly unique examples to try and take in their own singular purposes, their phrasings.

47

First, the great genius Raymond Federman, and
the opening salvo from his *Double or Nothing*:

*Once upon a time two or three weeks ago, a rather stubborn and de-
termined middle-aged man decided to record for posterity, exactly
as it happened, word by word and step by step, the story of another man for indeed what is great in man is that he is a bridge and
not a goal, a somewhat paranoiac fellow unmarried, unattached,
and quite irresponsible, who had decided to lock himself in a
room a furnished room with a private bath, cooking facilities, a
bed, a table, and at least one chair, in New York City, for a year
365 days to be precise, to write the story of another person—a
shy young man about of 19 years old—who, after the war the Second World War, had come to America the land of opportunities from
France under the sponsorship of his uncle—a journalist, fluent in
five languages—who himself had come to America from Europe Poland
it seems, though this was not clearly established sometime during
the war after a series of rather gruesome adventures, and who, at
the end of the war, wrote to the father his cousin by marriage of
the young man whom he considered as a nephew, curious to know if
he the father and his family had survived the German occupation,
and indeed was deeply saddened to learn, in a letter from the
young man—a long and touching letter written in English, not by
the young man, however, who did not know a damn word of English,
but by a good friend of his who had studied English in school—
that his parents both his father and mother and his two sisters
one older and the other younger than he had been deported they
were Jewish to a German concentration camp Auschwitz probably and
never returned, no doubt having been exterminated deliberately X
* X * X * X, and that, therefore, the young man who was now an
orphan, a displaced person, who, during the war, had managed to
escape deportation by working very hard on a farm in Southern
France, would be happy and grateful to be given the opportunity
to come to America that great country he had heard so much about
and yet knew so little about to start a new life, possibly go to
school, learn a trade, and become a good, loyal citizen.*

Federman, Raymond. Double or Nothing. Fiction Collective, University of Alabama Press, 1998.

I'm always thinking in terms of permission, and what this sort of sentence affords someone trying to figure out just how in the living hell they're going to manage to write anything. I read a sentence like Federman's and the initial impulse is to take from it a kind of permission. If Federman can open his book like this, if he can reach out to a reader and try, and trust them this way, and say listen, look, I'm going to tell you how I've perceived things in my life by writing to you in a way that might not seem welcoming, but it is welcoming, and if you'll give me your time I'll give you what I can, and I'll try and be truthful with you in terms of my sense of what writing can be, can do. There's a freedom, there's an indicator that we are free to exist with his work, and to carry his work with us, and carry it forward; to communicate and to commune with others in this sense because he did it, it worked for him, so why not? This is why reading matters to writing. I don't think you need to read a particular shelf in the library to be a writer, nor do I think you need to read a particular amount each day, each week, to be a writer. I do think this is something that the searching writer receives if they are reading and trying to find things that resonate. Even if you'll never write something like Federman's opening, even if you're not even all that interested in it, it does establish a precedent for how the novel can be opened, and what it might lead to, and that is a gift. You have to read widely for a time to find the things that are going to say this

49

expressly for you, but you will find them. It can be lonely, alienating work, figuring out how to write, and this searching in the shelves, or scrolling through Amazon, or making connections between writers and eras and publishers and the like, gives that process a necessary, social shape.

The next thing I think about when I read a sentence like this is the notion of bits of cigarettes, and spit, and pee, and whatever else, that coated the surface of Jackson Pollock's paintings alongside his paint, and ink, and blood and whatever else. It's a lived-in sentence, a layered thing, that compounds upon itself in a manner similar to quilting over great lengths of time. There's a consciousness in the sentence that's multiple — the opening, "Once upon a time two or three weeks ago," is the first indicator of it, being not quite either "once upon a time" nor "two or three weeks ago," but the shaggy combination of these. We're not, then, reading one quiet, somber individual's reflection on World War II, or its documentation, or its aftermath as it relates to writing. In a way, we might not even be reading one sentence, if that makes sense, but somehow a combinatory one. We're reading multiple iterations, multiple attempts at saying something that's too complicated to say right out, so instead he tries, and tries, and tries until the words seem to build atop one another and a unique register is found that seems to reflect the spirit in which the thing is being written. In musical terms it's a cacophonous sentence, not the bathing ritual of Stein so much as opening a quiet apartment window after an armistice has been declared in a large metropolis. The detritus on top of detritus on top of words on top of words on top of this consciousness, or consciousnesses, so that the end thing looks like ten things, and in reading it through the sentence second guesses itself as much as we do in processing the thing. It digresses as it needs to. Stability is abandoned in favor of the risk of excessive vulnerability, of overwhelming humanity, or being too forward, or taking a chance at something different. In a way it's a testament to the risk run by avant garde writers as it's a very difficult line to toe and an easy thing to mess up. Our response to such an opening, then, can be to sort of turn away, to say this thing doesn't look like things I've come to understand as the kinds of things I've come to expect to find here. Sure, that's perfectly alright. You can do that. I've done that. I probably do it every time I try to read *Finnegans Wake* and I'll probably keep doing it until I've either read the thing in total or shot a hole through it at the gun range. Something can feel too much, and that's OK. We can assume Federman felt his feelings too much when trying to sit down and yet again begin a book and yet again be positioned as a person in this field of great artifice, this prose-making, this book-making, this sentence-making, and trying to do something significant while also trying not to bore yourself to sleep.

So it's thrown in there too, that multiplicity.

Once upon a time two or three weeks ago, a rather stubborn and determined middle-aged man decided to record for posterity, exactly as it happened, word by word and step by step, the story of another man for indeed what is great in man is that he is a bridge and not a goal, a somewhat paranoiac fellow unmarried, unattached, and quite irresponsible

We have here then the movement from a man to another man, a story to another story, a time to another time. Every time we think we're shored up and settled into what this thing will in fact consist of, it's undercut again and we're left less and less stable with every passing phrase, even every word. This notion of recording, of a figure deciding at some point in their life that it was their time to record something "for posterity," seems useful in the larger apparatus of Federman's opening. If you begin, say, by mentioning that you're fifteen years old and don't have much to say, the form it takes or the eventual content must compel the thing alone — this fifteen year old better face great dramatic elements, some drastic something, if their narration won't be made to be the thing, although the notion of a fifteen year old not having much to say might formally lead somewhere interesting, i.e. the thing works because it's realistic in its desire not to say anymore than a fifteen year old might be expected to say. With this setup, though, of a figure deciding, in the actual substance of a sentence, that they are going to record this thing, that they are at a point in their lives when they have decided finally to record this thing, regardless of what might tumble out thereafter, your relationship to the ensuing material is such that we're not only more forgiving—of odd progressions, endless digressions, whatever else — but we're more attuned to the sort of thing that's going to ensue thereafter. This would seem to be why filmmakers, such as Bresson, and Scorsese and Schrader thereafter, have characters writing in notebooks and journals in their films. A reader or audience member knowing they're literally bearing direct witness to someone's interiority is at least going to try to do it. He's recording word by word and step by step. We have the decision to record, and then we have the movement to another man, the real content of this word-by-word account we're going to be witnessing, this man a bridge and not a goal, and thus we're settling into the sort of rhythm a bridge affords, or the rhythm of Federman's narration, word by word and step by step. A goal implies a stoppage, a finish, something up there we can look to and expect to reach at some point, whereas a bridge is perceptible from far off, and yet when you're on one your sense of movement sort of stalls, and the finish simply happens when it happens. A unique man, maybe, then, a bridge and not a goal. He is a somewhat paranoiac fellow unmarried, unattached, and quite irresponsible, and yet we've moved from the recording man to the paranoiac man so quickly that it almost seems useless to stabilize just yet. We can't settle, in a sentence — or for that matter a book — like this, it keeps us on our toes but potentially without pressure, as the humorous first words indicate a playfulness rather than a somberness.

And   then,   what   follows:

who had decided to lock himself in a room a furnished room with a private bath, cooking facilities, a bed, a table, and at least one chair, in New York City, for a year 365 days to be precise, to write the story of another person—a shy young man about of 19 years old—who, after the war the Second World War, had come to America the land of opportunities from France under the sponsorship of his uncle—a journalist, fluent in five languages—who himself had come to America from Europe Poland it seems, though this was not clearly established sometime during the war after a series of rather gruesome adventures, and who, at the end of the war, wrote to the father his cousin by marriage of the young man whom he considered as a nephew

Listing is a resource that will never stop providing things for writers. The listings here of the situations, the items in the furnished room, provides these brief crackles of energy that bring stuff to the brain, unexpected stuff that readers might not even realize they harbor associations with. The beauty of the listing of those details is they're then swept up into the experienced of what follows, details about the war, details about the life. If we get these elements entirely distinct from one another then it's up to them to do their job of holding our interest. Getting them in a list simultaneously elevates them and alleviates any pressure if we lose one in the shuffle. There's something, too, that I've come to think of as the FC2 style—FC2, or Fiction Collective 2, begun by writers like Ronald Sukenick, Jonathan Baumbach, as well as one of Federman's publishers — which is not limited to FC2 books but is something I've observed there frequently, the sort of layering that happens with phrasings like "lock himself in a room a furnished room," somehow, and I don't know that I understand it perfectly. That addition can almost function like a comma, a break in the initial phrasing. It's repetition, yes, but feels slightly less monotonous than the repetition we might get on page four hundred of *The Making of Americans*. It's second-guessing, digressing, like speech. The prepositional phrase "in a room" is arguably a bit humdrum, but somehow with that added "a furnished room" we're hearing the sort of voice that might be frantically leaving a voicemail after some ordeal has taken place. It continues, too, with something like "for a year 365 days to be precise," and continues with every iteration of this new figure, the old, no longer new figure, that's compounded upon. I tried writing that last sentence to reflect this style but felt compelled to add commas where Federman might've skipped them. There are ways of indicating to your reader that you're aware of the sort of cumbersome approach you might be taking to writing this thing you're writing, and I think this is one of the stronger ones. Much like a charming speaker might pause, check in with us, make sure we realize how the thing we're saying might tie in, or relate to them, before continuing. It happens a great deal in a work like Beckett's Molloy, wherein the vast majority of text you experience is one long — over one hundred pages and it's dense, being Beckett — relentless paragraph. Beckett, being the dramatist he is, and being so fixated on the fundament of language, gives enough evidence of this being a comic enterprise, a compounding, human, rambling, digressive, and comic enterprise, that it's a bit as if the pressure is off of you, like when George Carlin or Richard Pryor really start to riff. This is what stands out in Federman's opening. There's an energy to it, as if the book has already started happening before we got our hands on it. The repetitions, the layerings taking place function like field recordings at the end of a piece of music, momentary lilts that feed into and add onto the experience in a manner that's ambient rather than deadly serious and of the utmost importance. The writer is trying to write something, and needs to siphon through several iterations of what he's trying to write to figure it out, and so we're allowed to witness this processing and it becomes messy in the way true communicative efforts are.

Now   finally   the   closing:

curious to know if he the father and his family had survived the German occupation, and indeed was deeply saddened to learn, in a letter from the young man—a long and touching letter written in English, not by the young man, however, who did not know a damn word of English, but by a good friend of his who had studied English in school—that his parents both his father and mother and his two sisters one older and the other younger than he had been deported they were Jewish to a German concentration camp Auschwitz probably and never returned, no doubt having been exterminated deliberately X * X * X * X, and that, therefore, the young man who was now an orphan, a displaced person, who, during the war, had managed to escape deportation by working very hard on a farm in Southern France, would be happy and grateful to be given the opportunity to come to America that great country he had heard so much about and yet knew so little about to start a new life, possibly go to school, learn a trade, and become a good, loyal citizen.

It would appear a necessity to mention the **X * X * X * X**. It's one of the more recognizable components of this long sentence that's at the very least recognizable as an example not only of a long sentence, but of a sentence that's worth returning to and paying some attention to. The characters were also the title of a book on Federman, they've become a kind of synecdoche for his body of work. Why is it significant? Does it refer to a year? Does it refer to those who've been exterminated? These questions are sort of the point. It's left as it is, opened as it is, and it's the thing that we people reading need to reconcile, though more mildly than some of the more glaring moments in notable sentences in notable works throughout history — the Whiteness of the Whale, the green light on the dock, Hester's A… It's a thing that can fluctuate amid the surety of the rest of the thing. The references to that particular war, that particular concentration camp, localizes it of course. The slippery, slipstremy remaining components, though, these are less sure, these are more open, and thus the Xs and the *s point to that remaining openness, that remaining uncertainty, so as to welcome the openness of the remainder of the thing — I'd argue the immediate movement at the beginning of the sentence from one focal character to another accomplishes something similar, always *deferring*. The wave of information here simultaneously calls to the waves of information we're often piled with at the beginnings of long novels, as well as the likely redundancy of same, or the redundancy of these constructions we've come to expect in long novels or in novels of any length. It's as if Federman is saying "this couldn't be more important, and I cannot wait for you to forget all of it," and the brokenness of the remainder of the text seems to welcome it too. If details like this in novels are cast aside, what's left in the sentence that we're able to draw from? If the fictional - factual matters are so heapingly laid on our heads then what are we to take from this experience? As noted, it's not the batheable sentence of Stein, but it's certainly whelming, at least. An oratory? An address? A performance? Yeah. Federman's is an approach of one writer who recognized the need for breaking down the walls at the asylum where compelling fiction had been sort of locked up — not to put it too dramatically — and his method is one of over-saturation, of engaging redundancy as a structural apparatus in the context of the postmodern novel. A reader's eyes might sort of glaze over here, but possibly that's part of it, the way we glaze over at an evening of TV watching, until we've drunk some caffeine and *Paths of Glory* comes on at two in the morning and we're shaken by the experience. These would seem to be some applications of the sort of sentence at hand here.

Yeah.

At some point, before it became what it
presently is, on the website Twitter, the
artist and writer Brad Phillips talked
about a serve in a tennis match as though
it were a perfect sentence. Or rather, he
wrote that he wished he could explain—I'm
paraphrasing — why a particular serve in
a tennis match seemed like a perfect sentence. Tennis, either table tennis or tennis proper, seems a useful metaphor for the
kinds of things Federman is doing at the
end of this long, athletic sentence. "[T]
hat his parents both his father and mother
and his two sisters one older and the other younger than he," it's almost easy to
feel your head moving back and forth while
reading such a thing, following the writer's apparent trajectory while also being
at least partly mystified by the process
of its ensuingness. We get the digression
here, and the whole of life put into this
spot, like Stein trying to tell the story of a family, the history of a family
in its completeness, to its completion.
Rather than stopping, and matter-of-fact-
ly recounting just the facts as they've
ensued, instead the digression is used, is
needed, to harken to the speech act, to
harken to the process of actually trying
to do such a thing, and the rhythm of it
is quite like a complex tennis match at
its best, or more aptly perhaps table tennis at its best — this sort of more modest
thing, playful while being deadly serious to its greatest practitioners, vol-
leying back and forth and forth and back
in a small room with oneself as we try to
put together the matter satisfactorily.

ICH BIN

DUMM

I began writing with absolutely no sense of what a sentence could or should be. The notion even that I was writing "sentences" wouldn't have occurred to me, not really, not at first. My feeling was that I'd read some things that made me feel a certain way, and that these things had been about such a wide range of subject matter that probably the thing to do would be to sit down and passionately engage subject matter that led to more pages getting written and through this process I would ideally write something good. I would imagine most of us begin with a similar mindset, but perhaps that's not true. I had simply felt so taken up with certain reading experiences, and certain art experiences, and this notion that I could somehow tap into that myself was what affected me at first. It was a feeling, it was experiential, and although I knew that I was putting words together I didn't really think about that, or know to think about that. I also didn't necessarily think of that while I read something. Some things resonated, some writers resonated, while others didn't, but I wasn't zoomed in to the process in any capacity. I didn't understand, for instance, why going back to edit my writing could feel painful. I hated looking over it. I hated to be anywhere near it. I wanted to write something and then be done with it, get it as far away as I could, maybe even publish it and let somebody else figure out why it bothered me so much. I cringed to look at my own godawful stuff.

I didn't learn about the apparatus of

the sentence for some time after that. It took probably another year and a half or two for it to begin to settle in. I took writing classes and I tried to make my way into academia and I read more and more, but my own stuff remained relatively static. I might respond better to a prompt in a course, or get an idea about something I wanted to try, but in those situations it was the larger entity — the idea, the prompt, the moment — that seemed to speak to me rather than its composite elements.

It didn't change until one night when I lived alone in a studio apartment in Rogers Park in Chicago. I'd written a manuscript that year, prior to this realization, that came to be published as Postures, two or so years after that time. Writing that book, I'd make a big pot of coffee, bring the whole thing over to my desk, and start drinking it and writing, drinking it and writing, until I'd reached a point of completion and then I'd sit in the bath and read Jim Thompson, or Bolaño, or Frederick Exley, or May Sarton's journals. The process of writing was still primarily about the feeling. These writers I loved seemed to write with a great energy carrying them, hence the pot of coffee. Then I'd relax in the bath and drink som non-alcoholic beer and then I'd make a big chorizo sandwich and sit down to watch TV or something else mind-numbing.

I felt that what I'd written there was better than the previous two book-length manuscripts I'd written, but it still made me cringe to read it. I went on a bit of a dire mental trajectory after this, after which I moved home to finish school and leave behind the refuse of my stupidity back in Rogers Park. Before going home, though, I tried to write something where I was thinking about the language exclusively, to see how it might carry the thing thereafter. The story that resulted, "Bach-Mani-Brahms," marks the beginning of my paying closer attention to the sentences before me, rather than trying to evoke feeling, or experience, or anything else. Though in retrospect there's much I'd probably like to change in it, I mark that point as the first test case where I'd only thought about language, about sounds, about textures of language, and it began opening my mind to this bigger notion of writing sentences as being the sole focus of a writer doing anything.

The story exists in books I've got but I don't have a digital copy, so I'll include images here of my marking up the thing and trying to distill whatever it did for me then, and how it might do more for me now.

BACH-MANI-BRAHMS

[PRESSING ON] TONIGHT BECAME THE NIGHT, AND this night, and the best of all nights, commingled in a pile of sludge that was Midwestern snow out the window of a smooth-riding rental van filled with several other performers that make up the Marcel Chamber Orchestra's primary assets, and you are the pianist. You are the pianist, and tonight's concert in St. Paul might just as well be held in your third piano teacher's—Mrs. Cossell—basement because your nerves are the nerves of a young man whose fear is not the keys themselves but the prospect of the teacher looming so closely as to be holding a small black revolver up to your spine ready to 'click' and end your days here and forever in a split second. This sort of fear, ~~balanced irrationally against your admiration for the cool white keys and their highbrow black mountainous accompanying brethren seemed to~~ dwindled eventually into a child's dependence both on Mrs. Cossell and the piano itself, sitting after school daily to noodle away tunes and exercises by Bach or melodious anthems

Handwritten annotations:

I like the word commingled

Title works, it's open

repetition is nice

As an opener it's not bad in spite of an unwieldy story

Everybody must try second person at some point — It's fine

long opening sentence

long 2nd sentence

References pretty random basically illustrate I've no real knowledge of music

and nothings—original compositions—more akin to Philip Glass or the heavy-rooted minimalism of Giacinto Scelsi or Arvo Part. O.K.

Fuck yea — "Does anybody else smell that?" First cello~~, and first in your heart, Jeanie Wilcox~~ * says this with such disdain that you look around and try to hoist your nostrils up to detect the scent but the wintery Marcel days have left your nose as useless as your thumbs—arthritic now and only useful when playing if soaked ~~(a la Glenn Gould)~~ in Epson salts for twenty to thirty minutes before a show. Otherwise you tended to play without the thumbs and though this hardly proved advantageous it was funny and reminded you of a story you once heard about Glenn Gould needing to stack several TVs beside his piano to get through a particularly vexing Beethoven trill and the cacophonous white noise allowed him to proceed learning the section physically and the rest was mere recreation. Though you didn't have those TVs and your problem wasn't one of a lack of understanding or ability—rather extremities, plural—you remembered the notion fondly every time your piddling thumbs began acting up and screamed your way through ambiguous sections of discordant drivel, feeling entirely more relieved than the earlier days playing Chopin etudes with not a lick of interest in the following progression of notes.

* Shitty character name

tempted to just cross all of this out.

I've used this more than once I think. Way too "writerly"

I like piddling thumbs

almost too much but can work

eyeroll

"I'm serious, something really…*smells*, everyone…" And Jeanie's second utterance is the second to be uttered this entire drive, with a flutist and

I don't mind this but could as easily cut it.

clarinetist (married) sleeping awkwardly atop each other's heads and shoulders and a harpsichordist up front attempting to hold onto the Marcel classical station just long enough to reach St. Paul's sister station, this group wasn't much for conversation. You felt at the center of these individuals most days, a sort of sun to their ambling planets of noise and chaos that worked and reflected with them what you all hoped to achieve, some transcendent state of being to render the town of Marcel a distant memory and yet close enough to walk out of there feeling twice as at home as when you walked into the old church where you all practiced—perched just across the street from the courthouse, an observation you often chortled at, *forfeiting your place in one cell for another, and all that.*

You think of tonight as you pass by exits and cities along the way from Wisconsin into Minnesota and it reminds you of trips taken when you were just a boy. The bulk of your mother's family lived on that side of the Hudson/Stillwater bridge crossing and as a result you spent a great many holidays there, playing piano when you had a moment or taking extra time in the bathroom to read from books by Dylan Thomas, that sort of thing. You enjoyed Dylan Thomas but didn't necessarily understand every word, that seems so far from now, so distant as to almost be completely unimportant and yet as Jeanie sits there querying about the foul scent you each obviously smell you can't help but confide in the past for a feeling of connectedness with the universe and you welcome it as a hug from a forgotten love, the tuneless keys of your father's —Pramberger, morning walks throughout Marcel before nights teaching students who actually seemed interested in your insights regarding Gould's *String Quartet* or your combining the efforts of your three favorites into *Bach-Mani-Brahms* as a sad attempt to remain terrifically new and up to date, while retaining the musical sensibilities of Johann Sebastian, Sergei, and Johannes.

Film scores rattle through your head on long drives like this as you lean your forehead against the cool window ~~and relish it as the fresh side of a well-worn favorite pillow.~~ Bernard Herrmann conducting Robert De Niro through the streets of New York lets your moment become more than just a chamber orchestra trip from one place to another for a concert featuring other chamber orchestras and their wives—not much different from the bands playing in bars every Saturday night, you often reflect—and at the mere remembrance of the word "Wife" your heart drops down into your chest and the only salve proves to be Beethoven's seventh as it pounds into your eardrums seemingly from nowhere and the memory of Sara fades as quickly as it came. That is for the best, that is inevitably what must happen. And you let it go just that fast.

"Am I losing it here? Does anybody *smell that*?!" The severity of her whisper has now reached its peak and although Jeanie obviously hates putting herself out you understand this is little more than a ploy for

I like this

some attention because for each one of you this ride feels as interminable and useless as teaching *Ode to Joy* to a pale-faced sleepy-eyed group of nine year olds.

"Yes, Jeanie. We all fucking smell it. It's obviously the fucking driver. Just let it alone, will-you-please? Just let it alone." The words come from your lips before you've truly considered what their significance will be and you can't help laughing before they've registered with anyone else and the result is a quick gob of spit hurling across from your position to the headrest of the driver's seat and it melts in as a pat of butter into a frying pan before the sun's really up and the world is all quiet.

Tempted to hack everything else so that this one bit becomes the center

The van around you has now turned into an atmosphere of hostility and pure, visceral confusion. You think about your first years out of conservatory in New York and the promise in the world then. You think about Gould and his madness or Bach and his madness or Glass and his madness and you realize there truly is no grounding principle to any of this and you're all just sort of eking your way by until death or until fame and that's slipped as quickly as the thoughts of Sara back into the confines in your mind as you rest your head back against the window, finding perfectly the spot where it previously created a small—nearly microscopic—absence in the thin veneer of mist clouding every other panel in the van; but this absence is yours.

Although admittedly I feel like an asshole including an example of my own writing in this book I'm trying to write about writing, it happened that this story really did demarcate a turning point for me in thinking about language. I don't think it's a "good" story, but I can see that I had a vague idea, and thought I could try this thing I'd been curious to try at that point in my life, and it does seem apparent that the language is being given priority versus any of the more autobiographical stuff I would've been trying in my work generally at that point.

I do note that there's maybe slightly less cringe-inducement than there is if I open anything older than this story, where the most language-centric stuff you might get would be some really pathetic attempts at being cute or clever in my phrasing, or potentially descriptive stuff that proved accidentally interesting because I was focused on doing something else. I think if I could revisit it I'd try to do more with the title, which was an issue with a lot of my early projects. I like to come up with titles, and speaking from experience I highly recommend making note of any that strike you as interesting, as it's a much better feeling to have too many ideas than to have too few and be finished with something. I seldom felt like I'd actually earned any halfway decent title I managed to come up with, and this story would be an example of that. It's also worth noting that the phrase "Bach-Mani-Brahms" was something I walked around thinking and saying a lot to myself at the time, and might've been an early example of the kind of thing I tried with a sentence earlier.

After I marked up the story in my copy of *Marcel*, which is thankfully out of print, I went through and crossed out every line with a Sharpie marker, very quickly. This is something that's as useful for a writer, or any kind of artist, as the actual drafting, composition process can be. In fact, I'd argue it should be thought of as part and parcel with the drafting or composition process. Few things are more educational than throwing your work away, especially your early work. You've got to get comfortable with it as soon as you can, as the first few hundred pages will probably prove expendable. I also think there's a sort of solidifying aspect to not being precious about one's work, not overly sentimental. I don't know why that is, because obviously there are things I am happy to have written, and glad to have published, but I do think that if someone came to me and told me that I could wipe out all of it, and have one year to write one thing that they'd then put out, I might be tempted to do it.

The application of this seems two-fold. You're not just getting rid of the inevitable slurry of bad writing all writers must complete on their way to figuring out what this enterprise is going to mean to them. You're testing your subject out too, your relationship to the work you're going to try to do. If you write fifty pages about a summer when you ran around breaking into buildings with your friends, it'll probably hold some allure at least for you and your friends who will enjoy seeing these things recounted. If you're merciless, though, and finish that writing by taking the stuff out behind your house, and setting it on fire, your relationship to it will change, will lessen in sentimentality and attempts at being charming, giving way to something beneath what you thought you were trying to get out in the process.

I remember spending multiple years on a manuscript that was largely dogshit, that eventually became a dogshit book called *The Persistence of Crows* — a phenomenal waste of a title. I wrote it after some heavy experience when I'd finished my first year of college. I had an electric Brother typewriter and I wrote as consistently and aggressively as I could, eventually arriving at a massive stack of pages. Then, a month or so later, I went through the process of trying to transcribe these pages onto a computer so that I could start to figure out trying to send it somewhere, or whatever else I needed to do to see it turned into a book. I moved to Chicago and started at a new college, bringing the pages with me and transcribing when I had the presence of mind to do so. I finished transcribing and sent it straight to publishers. I had no idea what dogshit I had in my hands. I thought I was passionate, I *felt* like a writer, and this was enough. I found someone willing to work

with me as a sort of editor. I'd pay her
a bit and she would go through the entire
manuscript, marking things up and giving
advice. I did this. She was incredibly
kind and generous. I was nineteen years
old and in the habit of flushing my meds
whenever the mood struck me and staying
up too late and getting into fucked up
relationships and blah blah blah. My father printed out the transcribed document
and mailed it to the editor for me. Now
that my father's gone that picture of him
holding those pages is one of my favorite
memories. He'd printed it at his office at
the hospital with the help of some nurses,
and held it proudly, standing around them.

This editor went through the work, and sent
the pages back to my father's house, where
I went for Christmas break. I was so dis-
heartened by this massive manuscript cov-
ered in purple markings where I'd fucked
up and failed to do something actual—and
I feel shameful admitting this — that at
one point I put it out in the snow and I
pissed all over it. This would prove to
be a gesture more towards myself, my own
failures, than anyone else, as I did not
have a digital copy of her notes, so that
when I decided to do my about-face and
take her notes seriously, I was forced to
do so with a stack of pages that smelled
like urine and dirty snow. I was severely
mentally unwell at this time, and what's
worse I think I kind of romanticized that.
I don't think I had any other choice, honestly. The first person who'd even exchange
words with me was a paid editor who didn't

work for a press. This process reduces even the most mentally fit writer to a pretty miserable state, and although it's a very ugly stretch of my past I feel an empathy with that person and every writer going through it. Hopefully your struggles are less extreme or pathetic than my own, but we all go through it in some fashion.

Somehow, oddly enough, this experience also forced me to reckon with things. Facing that document every day that I worked on it, this kind of shameful secret text that I gratefully threw out page-by-page as I bore her notes in mind while editing, somehow I convinced myself this experience had real merit. We dream of what a writer's life might be when we're starting out. We see our heroes, and we try and tick these boxes, try to walk in their footsteps. It's impossible to do, however, so we must reckon with ourselves, we must become ourselves, and I think it took that to get anywhere worthwhile for me.

I still had no sense of language then, and when I transcribed it was a more robotic process. I finished it, on a computer my sister had given me, and I made the edits, and I did the slow, unrewarding work of trying to set this thing right. I also had a couple of very long phone conversations with the editor about her sense of the thing, which meant the world. After all of that, I think I saved a version I sent myself in an email, but at the end of that first year I rounded up all the pages, all these drawings and paintings

I'd done in my room, and finally that computer, and I walked down the large flight of stairs in the back of this apartment building I lived in my first year in Chicago, and I tossed it all into a dumpster.

I don't know whether I knew that I'd saved the manuscript via email, in fact I feel quite certain I did not. I wanted to throw everything away because even though I'd put all this work, these hours, into it, the thing itself was not working — it just wasn't really a book.

(The really sad reality is I kept at it once I'd found it again, and, like the story "Bach-Mani-Brahms," it wound up being published. *The Persistence of Crows* was published by a small press from Texas, run by a writer and his wife, and they made their books by hand. The story wound up in a collection, published after a long saga and mailed to me in a large books of books, maybe a hundred copies, by a publisher who did his best to sell his copies in turn, and some I think sold to friends and family online, but looking back I wish I'd had the presence of mind to completely destroy that manuscript, that one, as well as the one I wrote before both of these and published in a handsewn edition I left in coffee shops. Eventually I cut up the story collection and it came out as *Gag*, which is not necessarily as terrible as the original book, as it contains a lot of crossings-out and more worthwhile experiments. The first manuscript too I put through some digital cut-up resources and made it more or less insane and thus not as awful. Still, though, looking back, I'd happily do away with the vast majority of these things, which is why I think the notion of getting comfortable throwing your work away, or burning it, is not just informative but necessary, for if I were published at any larger scale with so many of these early projects, I'd barely be able to show my face on planet earth. They're mostly bad, and by sort of self-immolating at one remove in this way I'd have made the stuff that followed, more in this vein I've come to see as a necessity for the work. Just don't dump your pages in the snow and pee on them. Nobody wins.)

BOROS

Now I'd like to look at a sort of sentence that's sparsely littered throughout the world of writing, but most iterations of it seem highly important to what I think of as this "recursive" writing process, which I think this thinking about sentence-making would qualify as. These are sentences as sorts of circuits, that open something and close something later on, in their finishing.

The two standout versions of it that I'm interested in are from *Finnegans Wake*, and *Dhalgren*.

Finnegans Wake's circuit sentence opens the book midway through it — the sentence — and closes the book with its beginning. The whole sentence is as follows:

A way a lone a last a loved a long the riverrun, past Eve and Adam's, from swerve of shore to bend of bay, brings us by a commodius vicus of recirculation back to Howth Castle and Environs.

It's curious that the second portion of the sentence that we encounter in the book is a simpler, more playful phrasing — this language ends the book, and puts one in mind of the youthful, simplistic language that opens *A Portrait of the Artist as a Young Man*, which might not be Joyce's "literal" intention, but is a nice thought since we're thinking of this in ouroboros terms — where the first part we read is complicated and complex, pointing to the effortfulness we're about to be put through, only to arrive at this simpler sense later thereon. It's so jarringly pleasant in comparison that it's almost tough to reconcile these halves. "A way a lone a last a loved a long the riverrun" is just so wonderful to think, to repeat, to have in our mind, to have those bits of text in front of us, before us. It connects for me with Nichol's "A / LAKE / A / LANE / A / LINE / A / LONE," another wonderful sequence of language that seems to want to extract all potential from relatively simplistic wording. Joyce is giving us more than mere bookends, then, more than *story*. Reading *Finnegans Wake* for something like a story is a bit like setting fire to your hands to get warm. They're connected apparatus, as narratives and stories are connected to the text, but not in the usual recognizable ways.

It's much, much nicer to try and digest it in terms of its sentences, as at least there you can feel some sense of comprehending *something* (6). This sentence, on its own, ties the book together while pointing first to language, to wordings, phrasings, and then to waters as a theme for the book, then to biblical figures in Eve and Adam, then to the context where from Joyce wrote, of Dublin, of Ireland, then Latin, then this notion of an eternal return—the *recirculation* aligns pretty perfectly with the recursive writing herein advocated — and then too Howth Castle and Environs, which becomes Here Comes Everybody, H.C. Earwicker, and countless other things throughout the work. As a single sentence, it's quite impressive. Again the *Portrait of the Artist* sense of movement from a simplified register — which, oddly, *ends* the sentence, being the end of the book, but in fact begins it being the enclosure for how the book begins—to something dense, denser, referential, and more complicated. That opening, when it's reached — A way a lone a last a loved a long the riverrun—is again just so pleasant to hold in the brain for a minute.

While working through this sentence, looking at it and trying to conceive of it, I came upon this quote from Kathy Acker that seems to tie to Joyce's project quite nicely: *Literature is that which denounces and slashes apart the repressing machine at the level of the signified.* So, Joyce's war with the church, here. So Joyce's war with himself. So Joyce's war with the

(6) I actually think this kind of extremely minimal criticism can bear fruit, especially when thinking of an all-encompassing work like Finnegans Wake. Much as there are reading groups that only read a page a week of the book, thinking as a critic only about certain sentences in such a work speaks to the actual writing of the work in the first place, and thus seems sensible. It needn't apply only to critics, that's just the first place my mind went when thinking about reversing the constraint process usually employed to generate works, to analyzing them—for more on this, see Nicholas Rombes' criticism.

hospitalization of his daughter. The encapsulation and processing of this, its all-encompassingness—*denouncing*, on the one hand, the pieces of it, containing it, and *slashing apart* quite literally by making *this* sentence the enclosure for his final work; so the repressing machine then, of language (i.e. *the signified*) and all Joyce's gesturing at it. So Joyce's war with Dublin, with Ireland, with the university, with all universities, with academia. So Joyce's war here with the critic, the critical impulse, the need for critique, or the implied need. So Joyce's war with the icon, here, the sign, here, the referent, here, the signifier, here, the signified, here. So Joyce's losing battle with drink, with disease, with sight, with the apparatuses of publishing, with the apparatuses of writing, of being a writer, of sitting in a field and holding his hands over his tired, pained ears. *This* sentence, it need be said, is the only thing that could hope to contain the work it so happens to contain. A messy, a dreadfully or a wonderfully messy book or both, a book that I wouldn't necessarily hope to talk about or read in a conventional way and go out around the world championing, because I don't think it needs it. The sentence which contains the work's ending which begins **A way a lone a last a love a long the riverrun**... It's playful, and performative, and iterative, and re-iterative, to such a lovely extent that it's possible to say *look, just look here, just look and see here this one sentence, and make your muddy way through whatever's*

83

left of it contained there, and ingest it, and let yourself become sort of washed out by the language, and it can contain you.

While I'm as prone as anybody to hyperbolics when it comes to Joyce, or writing, it's important to reject certainty. It's important to shy away from any conception of certainty about whatever it is these writers seem to be trying to do. In the end, **I don't know shit**. Joyce, after all, worked on this book for well over ten years—I believe it's closer to seventeen—after working on another all-encompassing masterpiece, another masterpiece, and two other, briefer, masterpieces. He faced the courts for obscenity. He dealt with family trouble that ruined others similarly situated, and ruined him, and ruined those around him too. He continued on trying to *do* something with his work, his words, to achieve something perhaps untethered—there's no security in it, none at all, in fact it's the opposite, the far opposite of security, anxiety and angst without end. It's not hyperbole though to say that this sentence, curving as it does, contains the resonance of Joyce's entire living, the entire thing he seemed to devote himself to, this blur of it, this relentless blur of it, sliding as it does, holds all he managed to enact and more, and communicates the things a reader — or a writer — might take from such a practice, an enactment. It goes beyond permission, and gets at this idea of the applications of literature, of writing, of aesthetics, finally. Like other works from this moment the endeavor of Modernism — loosely defined, to be fair to them — was to contain as much of the world, as compellingly, as possible. This being because it would throw open the windows of potential transcendence to such degree that reading the book is a bit like opening the window of a speeding train and sticking your head out to take it all in. It's a work that rivals Kubrick's estimation of filmmaking as *writing War and Peace on a speeding train*— I'm paraphrasing some, I believe and thence the admiration Joyce had for cinema returns and feeds into the propulsion of this sentence.

It's probably doubly applicable here to think of these sentences that contain the books they find themselves within, as they represent projects whose sense of structure, of order, is within the apparatus of the sentence itself. If a film, for instance, opens and closes with parts of the same scene, the movement from one to the arrival of the other creates an inner logic that a more traditional narrative arrives at through other means. These sentences are anchors, then, to the messy sprawl of the enclosed texts, and Joyce's, with its opening mellifluousness, its biblical ambitions, and its use quite literally of that "recirculation," let it speak for the whole and not simultaneously. Possibly, as John Cage did—and Cage said he really only started to understand Joyce when he started doing this very late in life — the best we can do with such a sentence is to rearrange it, to repurpose it, to create acrostics or mesostics and read and write *through Finnegans Wake* as Cage did, and making it, remaking it slowly into this personal thing, a manageable, perceptible object only once it's been digested through our own thinking and we've figured out how we are going to approach it — again, zooming in as readers, thinking sentence-by-sentence, rather than looking for the professorial totality. Comparing it with even its own contemporary novels seems impossible. It's similar, in a reductive way, to the bible, this document that's opened, read piecemeal, across generations, and added to, and annotated upon, and mined, and questioned, and physically engaged with as well as intellectually, temporally, processing history through this work as it processes *its* history, stacked upon Joyce's table as his sight went, and he had to dictate, this eventual mass of text and ink and pencil-scratchings just like Stein's for *The Making of Americans*, two sides of the Modernist project and perhaps its twin poles.

A WAY
A LONE
A LAST
A LOVED
A LONG
THE RIVERRUN,
PAST EVE AND ADAM'S,
FROM SWERVE OF SHORE
TO BEND OF BAY,
BRINGS US BY A
COMMODIUS VICUS
OF RECIRCULATION
BACK TO
HOWTH CASTLE
AND ENVIRONS.

Now to look at Samuel R. Delany's approach
to the same sentential shape in *Dhalgren*:

Waiting here, away from the terrifying weaponry, out of the halls of vapor and light, beyond holland and into the hills, I have come to to wound the autumnal city.

I guess it's because of Joyce's precedent, but there's something so thrilling to me about the "error" in Delany's version (7). I don't remember where I read about it but I remember seeing someone extrapolate a bit from it and the points of disconnection that *Dhalgren* wallows in. Possibly Steven Shaviro's writing on the book, I think that's where I saw it first discussed, or saw the sentence put "back together" in this way. The "Prism, Mirror, Lens" that comes within the sentence but functions as a kind of chapter head is sometimes woven into the discussion. On one hand I'm admittedly somewhat hesitant to write about *Dhalgren*, though it's for a stupid reason. A year or so ago I got really fixated on writing a book about it, and in this spirit I reached out to Delany, and his response was kind of cold, and it really affected me. His response was entirely reasonable — he basically said that a lot of people have written to him about books they wanted to write about him, and sort of said *sure, but I'm not interested in engaging at this point in the process of whatever you're trying to do.* It hurt me, is all. I'd wanted my reaching out to be an acknowledgment of what a fan I am of his work, and to have it register as a sort of harsh reality check just threw me off. Every now and again I'll reach out to writers whose work means a lot to me, but I've stopped doing it so much recently because of a couple of similar bad experiences. I want to be able to write about *Dhalgren*, though, and Delany more generally, because his work

(7) Again I've got to mention this trouble with analyzing writing because I've learned since I wrote this that Delany hadn't read *Finnegans Wake* when *Dhalgren* was written. Frankly, though, that doesn't matter. They're both doing distinct things, and in Delany's case this idea of layering stories, or one story, over itself multiple times, is still very much a part of what *Dhalgren* does.

really is incredibly important to me, so hopefully this is a chance to open it up again. I want to write about it not just because it fits this type of loop-model for a sentence, but because, as in Joyce, it is a kind of totality as a sentence; the stakes seem kind of high.

This sentence, at least as I've reassembled it, because as with Joyce we have to assume perhaps it wasn't meant to be reassembled in such a way, is nevertheless so exhilarating to me. Doubly so when considering *Dhalgren* was, essentially, a bestselling kind of airport novel in its day. It's an ominous work, in the omen-ous way, and this blurry sentence, the reference to this sort of destroyed world, this mixture of its Edenic nudity and a kind of post-*Terminator* destruction, and this heroic figure stepping into the darkness, facing the cold world out there. Of course much of that comes later, but we have whiffs of it here. It's jarring, and effective. For a novel so steeped in indeterminacy it's important for *Dhalgren* to hook itself into the brains of its readers by other means, by these tendrils, "halls of vapor and light," "terrifying weaponry," "I have come to wound" — one of these methods, then, is the language itself.

If you were to unpack all the goings-on in *Dhalgren* onto several chalkboards it would seem entirely impossible to comprehend it, and part of that maybe is by design. It's a book about a future, that's steeped in certain moods from the 1960s and other vantage points in the life of Delany — a tendency which continues in the 60s-ness in *Through the Valley of the Nest of Spiders'* imagined future — and it devotes most of its attention to bodies, slowly churning their way through this space that's as indeterminate as the names and histories of the characters. Delany is asking a lot of his language, then, and is firing on all cylinders the entire time to accomplish something entirely other. Anyone who's made even an attempt at reading *Dhalgren* will know the language scatters and whorls into itself to such a degree that pinning down the author's "something" needing accomplished is tough, though no less compelling, and this sentence embodies much of what the words are trying to theoretically do, consisting on an open loop, disconnected with itself but still twitching and sparking at its ends. "[B]eyond holland and into the hills, I have come to to" is such a wonderful piece of I guess human errata, that migth've been created in the transcription of the text, or the recounting of something orally — via notebooks within the novel, as well — or some other means entirely, it calls the reader back to the beginning of the work— "to" meets "to" — but in a way that won't comfortably settle either. William Gibson called it a puzzle that doesn't want, or maybe need, to be solved, which is a useful phrasing. It's a novel, and a novel that's doing about ten thousand different things at any moment, and the restlessness of its characters is reflected in the restlessness of the writing in turn, which the repetitions, and the capitalizations, and the varied emphases, disrupt yet further.

Delany's feels less settled, I'd say, and Joyce's might be trying to rein in its unwieldy enclosed text, where Delany does offer us more graspable rock, so to speak, to wade through it. Both of them seem to split the atom of the sentence, to really disrupt the relative stability of their more simplified brothers and sisters. There are others that exist like this, ouroboran sentences, done at the level of the book, the story, the film, and otherwise, and it's a shape that seems to carry such risk of being heavy-, or ham-handed, in guiding a reading of the work, so these two stand out as examples embracing the openness of the sentence on both sides, creating something with language that's vital, while being abstract without providing annoying for doing so. It's a device that might scream I AM A DEVICE, but if handled with eloquence and trust in a little bit of uncertainty, unwieldiness, in the phrasing, its power does seem to hold.

Lastly, again, just these sentences:

A way a lone a last a loved a long the riverrun, past Eve and Adam's, from swerve of shore to bend of bay, brings us by a commodius vicus of recirculation back to Howth Castle and Environs.

Waiting here, away from the terrifying weaponry, out of the halls of vapor and light, beyond holland and into the hills, I have come to to wound the autumnal city.

RADICALLY

AFFIRM

SOME SENTENCES

OF

THE BREAK:

MAURICE BLANCHOT

Maurice Blanchot was perhaps the purest writer, a theorist of writing, who conceived of approaches to writing that made his actual texts that much more engaging because one gets to see firsthand his ideas about writing as an historical enterprise and as something capable of achieving personally-established effects—this is also a reason that my personal favorite way of seeing Gordon Lish's ideas about what writing can be enacted is to read Gordon Lish. Blanchot is an artist, then, and maybe the best distillation of the writer's writer France has offered besides Simenon, both obviously for totally different reasons. He opens up the possibilities quite literally in every utterance, and he's also a critic, a theorist, a philosopher, in the remaining good senses of each of those terms.

I thought it sensible, then, to look at some of his sentences, to try and delve into whatever it is that has made him such a compelling thinker for writers. These are pulled from a pretty scattered range of places within his work, and given citations as to what larger thing they're pulled from. It's worth noting though that any time given to simply reading the texts directly will reward anybody trying to write — because, unfortunately, this is a book I'm trying to write, I resisted the urge to simply copy and paste together only the words of others, though that book is coming into existence as a commonplace book called Sentences, and may someday come out. PDFs of Blanchot's works, largely in their entirety, is available via Monoskop, and in addition to that the *Station Hill Reader* is wonderful, as are the *Meridian: Crossing Aesthetics* books being published by Stanford University Press. Blanchot and others with a European sentential temperament often proceed in favor of acting as if sentences are already living breathing things as worthy of study as murder, or the human spleen, and these excerpts tend to reflect that. Why would you talk about linguistics when you could ruminate over death?

It is as if several of those who write, not knowing what will be dead tomorrow and what living in the realm of the aesthetic, and ignorant as to what mode of writing will be condemned and what saved, have become lost in rather cruel doubts from which only a number of certain prospects could've extricated them.

If I were to hazard an attempt at encapsu-
lating the situation faced by most writers as a means of figuring out their lives,
I couldn't come close to saying it this
well. This is the situation we all enter
into when we try to do anything, and making sentences especially, for the apparatus of the sentence itself falls in and
out of vogue as a sort of meter by which
you might access a reading public, just
one reader; people often want many things
from writing, seldom have they wanted
"just" sentences — the point being the
meter spits and slops itself up and down
by never clearly — there can be no clarity — the reading public can elude one as
much as it ought to, but the sentence will
remain, it has to, it's all it can do. As
everyone now knows, the vast majority of
Herman Melville's contemporaneous *potential* readers had to die before he found
anything like favor, along with the man
himself. We'd like to begin things under
circumstances that feel sure, because it
is awful, it can truly be *awful*, and for a
long time this meant that writers were terribly drunk for long periods of time just
to remain in that awareness, that *state*,
that comfort, that sense of surety of
their mission. It is such thankless shit.

Then, too, there have been those who
sought extremity in their days, and
this seemed to solidify this minor little task, this gesture of sitting down
to write, at least in comparison to the
stupid affairs they had, and the ways
in which they comported themselves.

Blanchot, this evasive figure—this *ghost*—
is talking about the horrors, the wars,
the stuff facing twentieth century — and
of course the rest too; and it is *cruel*—writers; and our doubts have only
grown dismally worse — there's no money,
no surety, no immediate audience and the
best-case scenarios involve going into
thousands of dollars worth of debt. The
sentence itself, though, speaks in turn
to the conditions it diagnoses and possible ways through or not. It's of course
worth noting that this sentence, as each
of Blanchot's that follows, is a translation of a sentence, written in French and
then garbled through the minds of probably several different individuals. While
that makes direct engagement with the sentence a slightly tricky thing, after a
certain point you just can't care, once
a writer resonates you must let it, in
translation or scrawled on a mattress pad.

Blanchot is speaking to the potential circumstances of all writers, "several of
those who write," as simply as I think he
might, and we can safely take it to mean
the pathetic lot of us. There's the literal sense of the living and the dead,
related to the circumstances then facing
the world — and thereafter, duh. The aesthetic, though, is its focus here. The
public mood is a labile thing, and writers are facing such a torrent of indiffer-
ence in any age that it's near impossible to know whether your little words on
your little pages will face living or dead
eyes the following day. It is an affliction,

a permeating thing, and answers elude almost
everyone. We know, again, of the expressly dire historical cases of someone like
Melville, who stumbled his way through his
stories, adventures, poems, encyclopedic
novels, obsessive Gothic sexuality, wrote
masterpiece after masterpiece only to find
himself unable to publish a thing without
paying for it himself, and ruined lives,
and children who wanted to erase his memory from their record, from the earth,
for his apparent tyrannical behavior, and
then his rediscovery only long after his
corpse went cold. You can't assume you
write for anything in *any* time, not really. You likely can't be afforded that gift
and you likely wouldn't trust it if you
were. The endeavor has to sort of happen with *you*, to start and end with *you*,
within this personal devotion to the language of the thing you're trying to figure out, your sentences, and it satisfies
you. Your work might face several deaths,
several indifferences of the "aesthetic"
present, and even thereafter might do
nothing for anyone for all time. This is
the thing you enter into when you begin
to write something rather than writing
any other thing at all, or worse, writing
nothing. You commit to *your* sentence, in
the sense of it being your life's sentence, and you try to undo whatever fuckups you've enacted there with fuckups
you'll soon forget in your enacting of
their opposition via yet more words, more
failing words, creating more sentences.

The sense of potential condemnation is

not a new sensation, it would seem. People, and writers especially, are often found waiting for the other shoe to drop, for good to turn bad, for success to turn to failure, or failure to turn to worse failure, more failure, insufferable, insurmountable failure. Not knowing whether our condemnation is forthcoming, or our regaling, we can only burrow our heads down into our coats and stand outside the window of the living and freeze, while wishing the same miserable fortune on everyone who would enter and encounter the thing — they are your brothers and your sisters, the whole of man — as they've already got it and it's the least we might do to share in that commiserative spirit outside of, beneath, running from, *life*. We exist, then, in our "cruel doubts," or we commit to the thing at hand and we risk the failure of our extrication from this circumstance. That's what's at hand, when trying to put something down and letting it remain there. Likely nobody will grab your shoulder and pull you up into that realm to be feted for all time, so all you can do is push aside the doubting and put something in its place—a sentence, I mean — any sentence, any sentence to rival *your* sentencing to life.

It's a worthy consideration for someone to engage in, as well, this sort of writing about the condition of the writer, or writing about the condition of the written, as it's the only way a person could reasonably hope to transcend it—I think, too, it speaks to the frequent preoccupation Blanchot has with death in works otherwise framed as being about writing; just as it's a useful therapeutic tool for a person to reckon with the fact that they will die, it's a useful thing for writers to reckon with the reality that they will, or at least they might, go unread, for just as we've all got to deal with the becoming of our selves, we have to deal with becoming the writer we're most compelled to be, readers or not. It's a weighty sentence, but doesn't feel over-long or too meandering. We understand, I guess, that the subject matter calls for this sort of expatiating, and similar to the narrator(s) of Federman, we allow for some digression in the name of find-ing a proven truth, as harsh or spare as that truth might be. Sentences like this — by which I do mean sentences *like* this but more importantly sentences by Blan-chot, because as you read him you'll see how consistently his sentences work this way, cover this material — are a help for writers because they speak to the task at hand, the universal state we enter, like Pollock's interview where he *denies* the accident of his paintings, that he's do-ing something *intentional* and it's up to us to reckon with that — the "readers" of Pollock — not necessarily him, at least not to every soul who encounters his work con-temporaneously, of now that he's long dead.

If crime is Nature's true spirit there can be no crime against Nature and so it follows that there is no possible crime.

Delany said that the "most important elements of any society are the artistic and the criminal, for they alone can force it to change." Living within a world increasingly stubborn about the prospect of change, not to mention improve, it's tough to put much in either. Nature is Satan's church. You would hope for your work to be in accordance with Nature, why so? You would hope for your work to be as close to the living, breathing world as you could possibly render it. In terms of recursion, recursiveness, I mean a sentence such as this. A syllogistic sentence such as this, arguing with itself, digressing as the brain does. That's the plight, our plight, the plighted state of the person sitting down and trying to do this. You're not trying to do this in accordance with the world as it's rendered in a glossy magazine stand in a major city or the colorful bookshelves of that season's bestsellers all retelling essentially the same thing and bearing little to no relationship to anything gutful one might hope to experience. This sentence speaks to that division, the fact that we are simultaneously trying to render something entirely artificial — steeped in artifice — while rendering something that's as close to the burrowed guts of the people who will read it and the future people who will write from it to make their own sentences. The world being a state of crime, Nature being a state of crime; there is no Nature, there is no world, there is no apartness, I mean, it's all right there. You can't defile nature, no matter how many vats of oil you drop into her, she will always win out — perhaps you can't defile pure language, which makes it troublesome. Do what thou wilt in writing shall be the whole of the law, hm. When I first read Sade I pictured him somehow transposed in space, among the stars, writing and yelling and frothing at the mouth, awful, sure. And Sade talked often of nature, or Nature, or the Nature of. It is possible to reduce things in life to these terms, these terms of abjection. It doesn't do a person, not to mention a writer, any good to think too heavily over *this* sort of thing, or they'll wind up committing more personal crimes than natural ones, and in the process remove themselves from the world of People in such a way as to be beneath Nature, buried under it never to have your yawps reach out through the bubbling tar burning your skull and rendering you entirely mute in the face of it — we have to consider the veritable *miracle* that even a stitch of Sade's words survived, such is true for Kafka too, perhaps even some of Blanchot, why not.

Everything is permitted, but that is a burden and not a freedom. God is what so everything is permitted. Spinoza's estimation of God is the thing. Nature is God and everything new under the sun is permitted. Every stupid defilement, every crime, I don't know. People trying to enact things in their pathetic living and getting nowhere. I am in a state of crime, anxious at the entry point of Nature, wilting there as the heavy wet snow falls down over my form, sinking further and further into the ground, the muddy ground, my boots becoming sopped with water and earth, my voice making no scream, and returning — ever returning — until I find myself forcibly shut up by the heavy, earthen boot of the natural world over my throat, and I am quiet, a silent writer.

Again, I like the structure here, working as a syllogism that simultaneously proves and disproves itself. If X is Y's true spirit then there can be no X against Y, so it follows that there can be no X — you might want to verify my math there. Blanchot's trying to understand and contextualize Sade, which is this sort of glorious impossibility writers enter into year after year, some—like Blanchot, de Beauvoir, Pasolini, Paulhan, Cooper — are more successful than others, but it still requires this inevitable shrug, this sense that you're either seeing something operating here or you are not, and I cannot hope to help.

Sade, finally, the very literal sentencing of Sade, the actual substance of Sade, the hundreds of pages written about what, Nature, about death, about crime, about abortion, about countless things visceral, bodily, disgusting, vomitous, noxious, annoying, ugly, pungent — the focus, perhaps accordingly, is on the things to which his name is lent, and I would not contest that this should be changed. Sade, after all, wanted to be forgotten in the end, two or three acorns on an anonymous gravesite where a tree might grow, his true sentence.

Blanchot is extrapolating something mor-
alistic in this framework, or rather amor-
alistic, but it's a curious thing too in
terms of logic, or essence, if crime sees
its true spirit in Nature with a capital N, if Nature represents crime's true
spirit, the world out there, thoughtless
animals and trees and floods and fires and
all this monotonous death and dying and
violence, if this is so, then there can
be no crime perpetrated on or in or about
Nature with a capital N, being this sordid state of criminality at its roots,
its guts — you can't get mad at a fire for
burning, as that is its nature. Then Nature with a capital N *is* this sordid, pure
state, a state that doesn't call for human
being, a state that doesn't *need* human being, but contains it, that will soon cast
off human being, that accordingly there's
nothing we might do that Nature doesn't
sort of contain, ingest, anticipate — no.

Let us imagine the last remaining writer, upon whose death, without anyone realizing it, the minor mystery of writing would also be lost.

Let us imagine the last remaining writer, like we might imagine the last avid practitioner of Timber Sports, like we might imagine the last fanatical admirer of the harpsichord performances of Scott Ross, like we might imagine the last diehard adulant of Poison Girls, or Honey Bane, or the sentences of James Purdy. Let's imagine the last punk, the last living member of Australia's The Victims, the last reader of the cryptic verse of Gilbert-Lecomte, the last writer of music reviews, the last practitioner of walking meditations, the last fucking Family Video. Let us imagine the last remaining listener of the Pink Fairies, the last reader of Mick Farren's vampire novels, the last Chuck Berry imitator left in the Wisconsin Dells. Let us imagine the last maniacal fan of certain types of barbed wire, of cereal, of sizes of coffee mugs, the last living member of the antique barbed wire society. Let us imagine the last remaining hacker, the last remaining philosopher, the last remaining member of Death Grips, old and infirm and filming himself in a retirement home, the last remaining sober person in California, the last pair of boots in your closet. Upon whose death, and whose death, and whose death, and upon whose gruesome death, without anyone giving a rotten shit, without anyone even noticing, without anyone even paying the slightest bit of attention, the *minor mystery* of all this humdrum rot, this lot, would then be lost, and lost, and lost, and finally lost.

People don't allow for simply, seriously, considering something nearly as much as they should. You're gonna die, I'm gonna die, you're already dead, *I'm already dead.* The conditional mode, just speculating and allowing people to speculate with you in turn, without rushing one way or the other, without that, to actually try and find something on which to consider your position — think about the condition there, in which you find yourself, with the pencil, on the laptop, see it through; eat it. For a brief moment this was one of the operative modes in France. Camus and Sartre and Beauvior, who didn't just write philosophical work, but wrote novels that often operated as stages on which to play out ideas, which Blanchot did, finally, and does here. Sartre, for his copious drawbacks, felt that his novels, and particularly the incredible, early novel *Nausea*, ought to be considered with more primacy than anything he'd done. Considering a scenario, "Let us imagine the last remaining writer," who *will* die, let us see, let us just look and see. The philosophical novel, that odd appendage, wherein something can be opened up that needn't be closed, like the conditional sentence here, a sentence that doesn't ask for easy resolution, from a piece that doesn't ask for that, but allows for someone to return to their mind in their consideration of it. It extends from the logic of the previous, which extends from the need to put something into language without seeking finality, determinism, or resolution. "Let us imagine," and suddenly the stakes dissipate some, we're no longer in the realm of the utmost seriousness, or if we are it's not being treated so direly. This is also the realm where things like suicidal ideation might creep in, where depression overtakes someone, or anxiety ruins their moment, and peace gives way to strained emotive reflection. Let us exist within the safety of this sentence, then, living and dying and dead and unborn writer, and not run to either side, not seek the human comfort of extreme consistency, not need to share things with this writer speaking, or the last writer living, only needing the sentence in which we've found this thing and the language there to hold the thought and accept its every implication, yeah.

It can be difficult to feel you're doing anything particularly solid when you're sitting in your room, turning sentences around, then turning them around again, then turning them around again. It's easy—and perhaps it's a part of the majority of writers' natures — to feel as if you're dumb, and useless, and incapable of doing anything substantial in writing, in sentence-making, in sentences, and quite possibly this is the norm, the primary mode with which we do what we're doing each day, or couple of days, or however we schedule whatever we're trying — there is no universal model. Thinking about things like this, like the *last writer*, and in their dying the last writer being abandoned, and nobody even noticing that it's happened. If you sit by yourself and you consider that, you

will likely either feel compelled to try
and do something significant in your sentences, or you will succumb to the depression of it, which is not unlike throwing
your work away — and perhaps it's a useful
thing to allow oneself to be occasionally
depressed at the state of things, and not
try to fight it so, and to wait in that
position until it comes back, if it does.
Most of us need that, a little light to say
you ought to keep trying what you're doing. I've come to start holding onto them,
little windows into feelings I had when I
first received these things that gave me
such hope about what I wanted to continue
to try and do — very often these things are
the sentences of other writers, writers
like Blanchot, and I implore you to *keep
these sentences close at hand*, whatever
they are, because those vital things, the
moments, distilled, pieced together, your
own commonplace book, that is your sustenance. We've got to consider a world in
which we have no audience, and no reward,
and nobody to encourage you, and nobody
awaiting the work you're going to try to
put out into the world, and after you've
considered this, you've got to think about
what you would like to say in that moment, in that spirit, and let that prove
to consume you. What I believe you'll find
if you persist in making your sentences
in this spirit is nothing less than the
profound warmth within your gut of a sure,
constant, quiet hearth, that will allow
you to *keep* putting these things together
— I am talking about *your* language here,
your sentences which you

are condemned to write — and laughing through it, really maniacally laughing through it, sentence-making in the spirit of someone who's allowed themselves to be put into solitary confinement with themselves, who's then accepted their fate of writing with bits of their excrement or blood on the walls, slowly filling them up with something incomprehensible and putrid and wonderful and pure.

"The Right to Insubordination," Maurice Blanchot, on the occasion of signing the Manifesto of the 121, denouncing the use of torture in Algeria and supporting Algeria's war as a struggle for independence.

[...] I shall answer that it is as a writer that I have signed this text: not as a political writer, nor even as a citizen involved in the political struggle, but as an apolitical writer who felt moved to express an opinion about problems that concern him essentially.

Wanting I guess a wide gathering of Blanchot's sentences, I wanted to include this, which focuses on the statement signed in protest of the events then transpiring in Algeria, because it highlights something writers are still struggling to reckon with: the notion of engagement, of being a public intellectual in the Gramscian sense, but having the presence of mind to engage with this sort of an ordeal without turning oneself into a spectacle. It's important to pare things down to their essence in such a situation, and even then to try and whittle yet further into the thing to make yourself perfectly clear — "as a writer […] not as a political writer, nor even as a citizen involved in the political struggle, but as an apolitical writer who felt moved to express an opinion…" — it reminds me of Don DeLillo's notion that it is a writer's role to *oppose* things, but it isn't adequate to do that in this grand show, this spectacle, it's an exact thing requiring an exacting voice. Even Blanchot, effectively more of a ghost than a writer, could manage this, and could do it effectively, when circumstances seemed to call for it. The sentence too is quite lovely, I can imagine an old solemn man speaking it, and thinking carefully over every word.

We know Blanchot as a writer, and this is the way in which he's chosen to be known, and that's enough, even though contemporary earth has sort of indicated it is not enough, not even close, it can still be enough. The text has to be evaluated, and the part of his identity which we are privy to is that of the writer, that of the person who sat down and tried to process his living in writing, which is all we should need from these writers, from any writer, from all writers, we should need the effort to take life and engage it in sentences, and if they've done that, the work is what we get, and this kind of restraint on his part seems admirable. The world is now lousy with writers who would scream at you about some vague position they've held for fifteen minutes, and it can make one nostalgic for a time when books, and the occasional odd literary magazine, were the only ways in which a writer was heard from. Blanchot's approach, too, is far superior to someone like Norman Mailer, who engaged constantly with his craft but did so in a pose of certainty, that pathetically American trait, and wound up spouting off nonsense 65% of the time. Portions of that 65% could often prove quite fascinating, or at least ambitious — *The Executioner's Song* is the masterpiece, and which parts he actually even wrote are quite unclear, compellingly so — but Blanchot's ghostly figure, haunting his life and works, watching it transpire until dying quietly, never really being known for anything but what he'd done in his little books. There's a purity to it you don't get with other writers, an honesty and a real humanity, that I think is rightly put in this, one of his fewer forays directly into the public consciousness on something beyond his obsessions, his writing.

"It is as a writer that I have signed

this text," not as *this*, not as *this*, but finally as an "apolitical" *writer*, who felt moved to express an opinion about problems that concern him *essentially*. At the root of him, the fundament. It's nice that it's above his status as a citizen but below some sense of his being anything like a political writer. The shifting identities that Blanchot casts off over the course of the sentence reflect the slippery relationship he has to authorship and narratordom throughout the rest of his work. Yet really, when we look at it this way, it reflects the indeterminacy of the relationship any writer is going to have with their work either way, and doing it this way rather than pinning one's identity down as X, Y, Z, etc., speaks to the relationship of engagement that's even *possible* for a writer, whether it's for this or that cause, there's always this shuffling deck of identities a writer is utilizing to put something down.

The development here of who Blanchot is, who he is not, what this text is, what it is not, and finally why he's driven to do whatever he's doing, there's almost a discomfort to it, not begrudging exactly but again trying to put his words exactly, and not waste our time. This sort of sentence, this sort of sentence-making, again speaks to this recursive strain, this idea that it is not our mission to accumulate and accumulate, so much as to chip away at, to circle, removing in the process of explanation, arriving at a satisfactory closure to take your leave.

Radically affirm the break: that is the same as saying (this is its first meaning) that we are in a state of war with things as they are, everywhere and always; that we are exclusively in a relation with a law that we do not recognize, a society whose values and truths, whose ideals and whose privileges are alien to us; that the enemy we face is thus all the more dangerous for seeming more indulgent, but is one with whom it is understood that we will never collaborate, in any way, and not even on tactical grounds.

118

It's tempting to take this as a writing dictum, as a possible means of approaching how a writer or artist might engage their subject at the most basic level—again, DeLillo: *oppose things*. You are in a war of attrition, and this war is being waged against the world as such, the languaged world, the world that is the case, and the points of victory are those in which you are able to directly affirm your person in all its contradiction, and these are the sentential moments in which the work will feel transcendent for you and for reader alike — or, to incorporate the American genius of sentence-making, William H. Gass: **I want to rise so high that when I shit I won't miss anybody**... an all-encompassing language moment wherein you put it rightly and nothing further is needed, not then, anyway. In writing, your position is often best-served if it's a position of pushing-back, of fighting back. Paul Thomas Anderson talks about *not* starting with just a blank page, so bring in your commonplace book of marrow culled from reading, from listening, from watching, bring in your enemies, line them up, and there you are. But it doesn't mean only the "fight," which is a reductive understanding of the actual struggles people face in living, so rather of finding new ways of engaging something, new ways of engaging the thing, be it linguistic, or in your material, and your relationship to it, or in your form. The stories have all been told. OK. How do we proceed? We attend to the microscopic, to the elements that have been glossed over by empire. Lish, here, puts it best and most efficiently: don't have stories, have sentences. Don't have operas, have notes, have scraps of phrase. Don't have paintings, have blots of red on a deep green sea, attend to the elements that make up the thing you're doing and find out what it's made of. Don't have songs, have noise. Resist the imperative of piddling notions of sagas, of epics, in favor of their bits of bone, their viscera, their blood, and when you've put the thing together with these elements, through sentence-making, through devotion to the sentential, you'll find the thing assembled has not, could not have existed in this way from any other vantage. You are opposing something, whatever it is, and this is how you address the task at hand. The singer of the wonderful band The Repos, Aaron Aspinwall, once published a fantastic, slim collection of stories called *People At War With Themselves*. Like his work in The Repos, it was a fantastic, infuriated work. The sentiment of the title, though, *is* what matters to me here, regarding this, because I think it is writing: people at war with themselves. People starting wars with themselves, people trying to reach the fundament therein and push back against that deepest inner thing. Or perhaps it's someone else. Perhaps it's the police state. Perhaps it's academia. Perhaps it's publishing. Perhaps it's the straight world, the square world. Perhaps it's banks. Perhaps it's student loans. Perhaps it's your parents. Perhaps it's your idols.

Perhaps it's grammar. Perhaps it's surety. Perhaps it's Gustave Flaubert. Perhaps it's Maurice Blanchot himself. Perhaps it's your medical bills. Perhaps it's your depression. Perhaps it's your OCD. Perhaps it's your gender. Perhaps it's your world. Perhaps it's the life you thought you were living. Perhaps it's food. Perhaps it's money. Perhaps it's waking up. Perhaps it's insulin. Perhaps it's the snow. Perhaps it's the drugs. Perhaps it's America. Perhaps it's France. Perhaps it's California. Perhaps it's Idaho. Perhaps it's people. Perhaps it's mankind. Perhaps it's God. Perhaps it's Philip Roth. Perhaps it's Gertrude Stein. Perhaps it's James Joyce. Perhaps it's marriage. Perhaps it's sex. Perhaps it's solitude. Whatever it is it's a process of finding these elements, engaging in conflict with them without an end in mind, and letting your sentences bleed from these wounds and rooms full of apparitions. Affirm the break, welcome the points at which you disconnect however briefly from every other wording.

So what it is you're doing when you're putting the first word at the beginning of a sentence is you're making a commitment, to finish it, wherever it should wind up, and you're doing this in search of the language that exists within you, the language you've digested from the world but also the language that predates you, the stuff from your parents, and their parents, and the words that have echoed across time to arrive there in your anxious stomach. You're writing something that doesn't exist, even if the wording exists, it hasn't been written this way, from this perspective, and the only way of having it out is to go through this process of digging, and transcribing, and slowly making this thing that could not otherwise be made. The surest way to pinpoint this thing is to position yourself as breaking off from the normative mode, releasing yourself from the strictures of your contemporary and trying to push for something truly honest, something burrowed deep that might not want to be released, that might not give, that the square world wants to tamp down, and be sure it's kept at bay, and that's the thing you're opening yourself up to in this process, and it's a nauseating process, and it's frightening, and it won't always work, but you're summoning up the energy to do that thing and find that language and position it against some dominant orthodoxy, saying that your world and your sense of the world exists, that it matters, and that you're going to assert it alongside others who you'll champion and support in their attempt at same, that you're bearing witness to the rift that exists between the individual and the world, and not only are you doing this but you're raising it, raising its potential among your kind, you're asserting its necessity and you're pushing back against the breakage to find some other way, some other thing, some other world.

What you're doing is not a search for perfection. What you're doing is an acceptance of the fact that any sort of

perfectibility is dead and gone, long behind you, isn't even interesting. It's
like Cioran's idea that there's no sense
in committing suicide because it's always
too late. Once you've accepted the idea
that you are burdened with your humanity, the work you're going to do with that
is about a kind of forward movement, of
throwing good living after bad until you
find yourself spent, written out, a corpse,
with time. Perfection, then, is not even a
desirable goal, not when it comes to language. It's as useless as imagining a perfect human being. In language, anything
muttered after quiet is fleeing perfection
for something else, something different,
and it's this difference into which every
sentential writer moves, piece by piece,
with time — it should be noted here, too,
that this needn't exclude verse, Mary Ruefle
is one of the reasons "sentence-making" as
a phrase began growing in my mind; so even
if your sentences have line breaks, the
approach still applies. There is no perfect sentence, then, no perfect register, but there are holes within the cave
you're walking through that are worth digging out. Possibly some offer you salvation, possibly others something worse,
possibly others a good warm swim, a bath,
like Stein's sentences. This is the practice you're undertaking and it's an im-
perfectible one. To attempt openness,
then, is the first part, and then you're
tasked with making your way through
the language that happens to present itself there with yet more language that will
jut up against whatever preceded it in a

way that is not perfect, but brings about a kind of satisfaction that tells you that you are using your language effectively, your innate language, that you are mining something that is good and possibly even pure, being laid upon its surrounding words, or wounds, or worlds, and the effect is that of putting together a quilt, but doing it slowly, letting certain strands of fabric or yarn or thread wither away, and compounding on this effect enough that the effect on a person reading this kind of thing is their engagement with the language of a people, of the people you've been in your life, in your living, so that words ring out, and tumbling phrases flit and push into one another again and again.

ANOTHER

O   P   E   N

I   N   G

SENTENCE

I wish either my father or my mother, or indeed both of them, as they were in duty both equally bound to it, had minded what they were about when they begot me; had they duly considered how much depended upon what they were then doing;—that not only the production of a rational Being was concerned in it, but that possibly the happy formation and temperature of his body, perhaps his genius and the very cast of his mind;—and, for aught they knew to the contrary, even the fortunes of his whole house might take their turn from the humours and dispositions which were then uppermost:—Had they duly weighed and considered all this, and proceeded accordingly,—I am verily persuaded I should have made a quite different figure in the world, from that, in which the reader is likely to see me.

There's something in digression that literature is able to offer, that really no other artform can hope to reach, and Sterne is perhaps the greatest digressor who ever lived. Digressive films or TV series will feel tedious — the ones that stop, look back, dwell for a moment and then balloon in some other direction, or those late-in-seasons shows that starts incorporating musicals and "Sliding Doors" episodes. In literature, though, not only is the reader able to slip into the fold of a digressive thought, they're often compelled by it and moved to keep reading, and if not that then they're at least far more forgiving in their search for whatever else a text might offer them. This one, drenched as it is in birth, bearing, and the parental disparity between what conditions we seem to have been brought into the world to meet and to react against, is one of literature's great digressions, an unreal digressive sentence. Here we see Bernhard, Roth, Céline, Paul Beatty, Kathy Acker, and the precursor to any great rant ever written. There are moves being made right away that open the field for this sentence, the language of "I wish *either* my father *or my* mother, or *indeed both* of them, as they were in duty *both equally* bound to it," it opens up the sentence by not putting limitations on its occupants, and rather than looking for absolute clarity as to who is being referenced or addressed — or blamed — and what their role in the apparent undoing of this child. Instead the unclear is favored, the abstract, the rambling, in what could be seen as a tandem effort to highlight the linguistic character of this narrator, while also embracing that slipperiness that will carry through the remainder of the text. He's a great liar, a great orator, and as either of these things he wants the emotional weight of his commitment without the onus of any consequences in turn. It's small, though, to see the prime goal of such an ambling sentence as the establishment of the voice of a character. It does accomplish that, but it does infinitely more to one's experience reading and writing such a thing and undoing expectations for what this will in fact consist of. This is an issue with digression, from the perspective of readers, it can prove boring, like watching an extremely long, slow, apparently simple performance by a single figure, sitting on stage with a guitar. It seems to require a readerly submission, but in exchange this kind of digressive writing can captivate the brain so completely, there's nothing like it.

A writer in this mode is not necessarily interested in finitude, in bare clear light of what is being expressed, but rather the humanity *within* what is being expressed, the human spirit, so the effort elides what might be seen as a perfection, in favor of the spiraling, dwelling nature we tend to have in our actual thinking. This is another aspect of literature that isn't as readily apparent in other artforms. I don't know that I'd call it a transmission of how consciousness feels, as there's music and image and feeling and scents that crop up in the feeling of a given day in the life of a human being, but in terms of a linguistic representation, of the voices in our heads, in the things we sort of puzzle over and gnaw at throughout our lives, that's something that's *right there* with literature whereas it's limited or dulled in other artforms. I think the difficulty can be that literature's apparatus, the book, has proven less addictive than the abundant other forms of art and media and entertainment, but there are undeniable pleasures apparent even in just this opening from Sterne. It's also a testament to what we're trying to do as writers, which is to not make writing more like film, or more like TV, or even necessarily music—there are overlaps between these things, of course, but distinctions are important when thinking about the fundamentals—but to embrace writing for what it is, and embrace texts for what they are, and sentences for what they are. The present world's apparent disinterest in literature isn't even all that measurable, for every purchase of a book there's a haunter of libraries, for every novel-reader there are Substack readers, for every student of the classics there are sci-fi or crime fiction addicts, for every e-reader there's Granta, the New Yorker, the Paris Review; and this sense that it's dying off makes as much sense as someone in ancient Greece throwing away their storytelling inclination because someone represented the hunting of a boar more effectively in paint on a pot. These things exist in simultaneity, and almost always have, and they fill and fulfill different needs and interests for different people, and always have. Sentence-making, especially in the manner of Sterne, or Blanchot, represents writing comfortably removed from the concerns of other artforms, something unto itself that puts its stake in the language at hand, and attempts to convey consciousness adequately to the purpose of the work— here, the digressive, the sort of Holden Caulfield second-guessing, or double-speak, the meandering look at a young person born into the world and reflecting directly the positions and ambitions of its parents, they feed into the serpentinous sentence and give it its shape.

The focus shifts with every added word, so the effect might be closest to listening to a piece of music with slight variations in their emphasis, compounded upon one another like different pieces from the same film score by Philip Glass — I'm aware I dissuaded from this tendency of trying to make writing function like the other arts, but in this case I'm looking for an effective comparison, rather than trying to say this piece of writing is modeled on Glass, or Sterne is foreshadowing atonal music or something like this. As an introductory effort of creating problems for oneself, and then solving them, or making promises from one sentence to the next, this represents one of the louder cracks I've seen.

The whole of the world could be forced into this jagged shape of a writer's consciousness, and thus when it began to come out and shape itself the sentence got jagged, and it returned upon itself, and it tried to do something that wouldn't shut itself up and give itself over to bland recitation, to some sort of moral education. Writing at its most searching is a recursive act, something wherein one sentence compounds upon the next, and the writer returns again and again to the premise they've put forth, and tries to undo themselves with each movement not just in terms of crazed action or dialogue — though this can be part of it too, sure, *yes* — but in terms of the entirety of the thing they're doing. Begin, begin again, return, return again, and push yourself within this thing you're fashioning to find its movements.

This "person," in this sentence, dwelling over their parents, dwelling over the conditions into which their parents shat them, dwelling over the language available to represent this, they contain the vicissitudes of their moment, of "rational Being," and of "the happy formation and temperature of his body," and the fact that it's all contained here, in this punctuated sentence, this sentence filled with returns, proves to entrance, and to not bore, and to welcome in whatever judgment, through these breakages, be it in dashes, semicolons, whatever, the thing seems to need to keep on, to continue, to fully articulate right off that, before this figure, this voice was even *born*, it was being fucked over, beaten down by life, it's all right there.

A SENTENCE

FROM

IN THE WORK

ELSEWHERE

"Shall I admit that more than once I wanted to share that kid's sleep— i.e., to be fucked and fucked and fucked by him until I bled?"

I remember pretty clearly the first time I read it, in my copy of *Partial List of People to Bleach*, just after reading Gordon Lish's wonderful, frenetic introduction. I read this sentence, and I started to laugh so hard, I was consumed with laughter as I ran upstairs and read the sentence to my sister, and some of its surrounding sentences to offer context, and I don't know whether she laughed, and I'm certain she didn't laugh as I laughed, but I had found something so pure, this rare cut diamond in the middle of this incredible, linguistically dense work, and it made me feel so warm inside, so happy, so filled with laughing — I've held onto that moment for as long as I can.

"I came to language only late and only peculiarly," begins Lutz in "The Sentence is a Lonely Place," and describes the absence of a particular kind of language as an almost felt presence throughout adolescence, into teenage years. Then attempting to put into words the shift that happened, why it happened, and how it might work as a framework for both writing and reading. Writing, here, an arguably visceral and exacting thing, a language as innate as you're likely to find, rendered in the world for us to read, but it is an interior language, a thinking presence, an interiority. It's also a kindness to the spirit to know that Lutz arrived at the work over time, through graduate school the struggle continued, and it's a continuing process, and thus perhaps it's accessible, if we pay attention to our own interiority and these snatches of language offered there.

Reading these writers — the "Lish" writers — or at least certainly reading Lutz, I like the idea that our words, our sentences, the actual language we manage to put down in our lives are far better than any autobiography could hope to be. The chosen moment, the opportunity taken to speak, to write, to share something, but not this constant vomiting thing, not footage, not a biography. This stuff is plucked, and worked over, and then it's given out. Thinking of it rather as a sort of rendering, an autoportrait, a distillation, where our internal language has been put out in sentences across these works, and someone can tap into that vein long after we've gone. It's closer to who we've been in our living, and reason too that someone like Stein seems to revisit and return to things over and over and over — "to be fucked and fucked and fucked by him" — across her projects. She's dropping bits of paint, and sweat, and blood—"until I bled"—from page-to-page.

This sentence — I often think it is my favorite sentence — to return, or begin, or return or begin again, speaks volumes about the sort of effect a human being might achieve in their writing, a capaciousness, a capacity, and the sort of effect this will thence have upon a person engaging with such a work as a reader.

Shall I admit that more than once
    I wanted to share that kid's sleep—
        i.e., to be fucked
            and fucked
                and fucked by him until I bled?

This is a joyous sentence, I think, a celebration of the feelings that can amass themselves in the guts of people who live day, after day, after day trying to accord themselves with some sort of artful principle, or the prospect of an art that might weasel its way into the days of our working lives. Doubly impressive is it's a question. In stories, questions can add, compound, as digressions do in Sterne, or Stein, or any adequately angry narrator. They can be put without question marks, or with them, sure — can't they. "Shall I admit that more than once," yes, *yeah*. "I wanted to share that kid's sleep—" it makes me think of death, which is neither here nor there, but speaks to the nihilistic endeavor, the desire, to be canceled out, to be halved, to be fucked. I want to share the sleep of another, I want to be lying there, just like the Faulkner story, I want to be lying there with this kid — dead or asleep or what, and is he sleeping in the class? — whoever it is, some student at a community college, and to share sleep, a concept that explains itself away as soon as it's said, and effectively so, without any sap or sentiment, just the thing itself being put there, making way for the visceral stuff to follow. And then the wonder: "i.e., to be fucked and fucked and fucked by him until I bled?" which speaks to speech and does away with it in fine abrasive spirit. We are dealing with cumbersome stuff, in language. We pull and we push these things and often they're as stubborn as we are and they refuse to move from our

our consciousness and out into the world. This repetition, then, is not simply there for its own sake, as a mere act of repetition, but an act of anger, or pushing back against the stubbornness of language, as well as the sort of brilliantly digressive thought-rendering that's exhilarating to follow. Even that doesn't really get to the heart of it, because as a writer, in the context of this story built of sentences, each as striking as this one, we experience a humanity distilled to its utmost in this rendering, and the release of laughter, or great relief, or curiosity we cannot bear is its gift.

"The words I loved were in a different part of me, not accessible to the part of me that was required to make statements on paper," in the beginning of Lutz' essay the first observation that's made is of the actual materiality of words, that they are concrete things that are rendered out into the world, whether written on a page or spoken aloud. The process then is about discovering where these words, *these* phrases, , these resultant sentences might be accessed within a person through the repeated efforts of reading, and writing, and trying to embrace the notion of the word as a tangible thing that can be manipulated, rearranged, reformed into things that previously might not have existed, and certainly hadn't existed for you. The words that a person comes to love, those of writers we love, or moments staring off at a sign on the highway that we love; they remain stored up someplace that doesn't leap to the foreground when we're sitting down to write something, not immediately. The feeling of writing is the feeling of most any thing, and in this instance it would seem to be like therapy; you can *fake it til you make it.* This is why so many writers talk about sitting down and transcribing the work of writers they admire. In part it's about feeling yourself making this thing you've built up in your head — if you can convince yourself you're effectively *making* these sentences the same way that Such and Such did once, then you can start to feel confident that *you* might make similar sentences in your own time. The other aspect of it that's important is the beginning of a lifelong process of drawing on this well wherefrom words come, but are also always elusive, until we do that work of hacking away at its surface of ice and we reach into it and pull things out for our sentences. You fake it, or you imitate, or you scream, or you copy and you copy and you copy, and then you arrive at this place where maybe things come more easily, more readily, and the part of yourself that at first felt different, inaccessible, suddenly becomes as tangible as Lutz' realization of words in their concrete state as things within the world — the very same way that, even as far back as Freud, someone grew *more* communicative and most importantly more *meaningfully* communicative as they engaged in talk therapy; the very same way that a seasoned member of AA might know the particular meeting they should hit if they're angry, and need to vent, or if they're sorry, and need to repent, it's a thing that builds, because of your work.

The sentence, too, as a *place*, rather than a mere construct of communication, a noun-phrase and verb-phrase, or a subject-predicate, or a subject-predicate-object. A sentence as a *place*, as a world to occupy, as a reason for visiting and the context entered into when you're doing your visiting. A sentence might be a room you enter, and the scattering of elements can either be rendered with such particularity as to differentiate the room in which you write from the rooms in which hundreds of others write, or things could become Proustian where the room is not satisfactorily rendered until every single stitch of information is accounted for, and the library where your childhood was spent between the legs of your drunken, decadent parents is set up into this wonderful menagerie of sounds, smells, sights, names, objects to touch, things to witness.

I've always felt psychoanalysis proper to be the most amenable to the practice of art and writing — equally dense and informative, equally rich and frustrating as living the language of living. Our memory of a barber's striped pole might draw to mind feelings of heft, and warmth, and the strange smells of menthol aftershave, and cigarettes, and the barber downtown where you used to sit while your father got his hair cut. We might call the room *paternal*, or *brown in smell and hazy in sight*, or *abject, and male.* Whatever the object is, be it a room or a sentence or a cup, our relationship to it can be mined, even if it's something with which we have no apparent, or immediate, association. When you begin the process of addressing the thing, the object there, these associations arise, and generate language, and it's up to us then to continue to pull at those threads, to find its more perfect distillation in the process of revising — only ever more perfect. This approach of highly-focused, sentence-level writing, sentence-making, might skip the Kerouac scroll or the cutups of Brion Gysin, for by following our inner linguistic nature, our intuition, we can make associations, and stitch them together piece-by-piece, so the end is just as atypical, as non-normative, while remaining intuitively connected to readers and their own sense of language. Jason Schwartz is someone in this vein that's often quite like Lutz, though with Schwartz the connective tissue has been severed, so the associations, the linguistic signatures, the idiolect, are more starkly put.

Lutz did so much for me in all of my doubting and concurrent certainty that I was always a pretty dumb, unliterary, artless person, and I had no place whatever in trying to write anything at all. Lutz isn't dumb, but doesn't feel unnecessarily wordy or "literary" either. Where there seemed to be a pressure to act, to appear, to present yourself as an artist, Lutz wrote in a way that felt indifferent to anything but *its own* need for existence, and abstained largely from any kind of actual appearing in the world or pushing the work in such a way. There is, too, the inescapable notion that when we try to write with any authority on a subject our best recourse is to begin from within our own minds and experiences. I didn't read a lot when I was young. I snuck by in middle school and was put into a program called Smart Start in high school where I'd be able to continue to sneak by, somehow, in a sanctioned manner that looked like a real endeavor. I "tested out" of high school after getting out of rehab. Sixteen, seventeen, undergrad, grad school, I read some more and more, but the relationship to that elusive inner language isn't something that I figured out for some time. It needed to enter me, perhaps as a virus from outer space, but it only happened with time, it only happened after I remained open to the reality of my own looming failure, and to the sort of slackerdom-cum-obsession Lutz articulates across her work.

Once the words begin to settle into their circumstance in a sentence and decide to make the most of their predicament, they look around and take notice of their neighbors. They seek out affinities, they adapt to each other, they begin to make adjustments in their appearance to try to blend in with each other better and enhance any resemblance. Pretty soon in the writer's eyes the words in the sentence are all vibrating and destabilizing themselves: no longer solid and immutable, they start to flutter this way and that in playful receptivity, taking into themselves parts of neighboring words, or shedding parts of themselves into the gutter of the page or screen; and in this process of intimate mutation and transformation, the words swap alphabetary vitals and viscera, tiny bits and dabs of their languagey inner and outer natures; the words intermingle and blend and smear and recompose themselves.

This is, at once, what I'm talking about
when I talk about a *passivity,* an *openness,*
and it ties to this bigger notion of
writing as a meditative, or therapeutic, practice. On the one hand it is
a thing of the will, of continuing
on, of pushing on, but the actual engagement of that will is a sort of
subdued mindset, a free associative
thing that allows these sentences to
get made in the first place, and then
comes this openness to the process in
revising one's work, drawing further
connections that have been hinted at
or begun or opened up with the first
act of composition, but which settle
into their certitude with the ensuing
act of viewing one's work for its tis-
sues, its connectivities, its blips or
bits that a first draft begins to chip
away at, like a block of ice we've made
initial cuts at with a chainsaw, and
which we're now beginning to etch away
at with a small file and chisel. The
world offers us a coldness as writers,
a disinterest, and it's then incum-
bent upon us to turn it into something
worth looking at again, and again,
and again, until a slight melting occurs, the readers' hands have warmed
the thing just a bit so it holds its
shape, but the iced, white coating of
the block has given way to something
clearer, and the relationship there
is the process of writing one's work,

then revising one's work, then handing over the work to a reader who will make their own adjustments in turn, their interpretations. We trust in the fluidity of the thing. We trust that if we're going to be there, working with it, kneading words into sentences and turning those sentences around, around, around, that what might be offered back is the fulfilled thing, the realized artwork, that we've dug our hands in to shape, and finally it's there.

This is a question. If we're getting into this because we've got some sort of an abrasive relationship with living — and it is *any* abrasive relationship, abrasive relationship, it needn't be qualified — and if we're doing something that is sort of therapeutic in its own sense—being art-making, sentence-making—then this is a guiding principle we can learn to put into use. The one is fed by the other, and their inconsistencies ironically only add to that process. Something that took me some time to realize, though, is that the acoustic-heavy stuff, the sonic sentences, the meticulously-crafted sentences, these are just *one* possible iteration of this sort of devotion that one can employ. We've got to think too of the Federman sentence, a terribly messy thing whose very nature goes against being exacting, with no overt tendency to solidify its syntactic menace with enhanced written English. Federman being Federman, the result is a sprawl, a messy, playful sprawl, but it's no less sentential or sentence-focused than Lutz, than Lish, it's just employing different aspects of that same sentence-making process. Think too of the differences apparent even within *one* author's oeuvre, take Melville again and the vast divide between the all-consuming sea of *Moby-Dick* and the soap opera dramatics of *Pierre*. Not only did the same author make the sentences of each, he made them relatively close to one another, containing as he apparently did some guiding internal light that led to both, and led to still other places with *Bartleby*, *The Confidence-Man*, and *Clarel*. This is one thing that does seem to get lost when someone limits their reading to a particular strain of sentential stuff, you start to think that communicating in that particular register is the only solution a person devoted to sentences might reach, but as you gravitate outward you become aware of infinite different approaches, each more unique and deeply-hewn than the next. The ends vary entirely, but the making of the thing boils down to that attention paid, and it's there where sentence-making occurs. I don't think that this is an elitist practice I'm advocating, I'm only interested in thinking of the sentential only, but I look to the sentences of any writer as potentially drawing from this internal sense, this unique language. The therapy model here, too, fits, as one therapist applying the exact same essential methods across four different nearly-aged depressed women will see four drastically

145

different situations. There are writers who might be more amenable to sentence-level analysis, but I'm equally fascinated to see someone pick apart the sentences of Lee Child, or Thomas Merton, or Sistah Souljah; and when we think of the attention that's been paid to mere scraps of Shakespeare's language, it's a wonder more zoomed-in critique isn't utilized more consistently. Of course I'm speaking largely about the *writing* of one's sentences, but I hope its application extends beyond as well.

I think it's good to look at the sentence as an object, much in the same way it's become incredibly important to think of the book as an object, or the story as an object, or the poem as a kind of object. We tend to use a more limited sense of what an object is when we go about our daily lives, forgetting it's referring to really any old thing, and when we take our conception away from the abstract, the sort of floaty in-between of being part of this thing we're making that isn't quite an object, or entity, I think we lose out on some of the potential, much in the way we lose out on the potential of a truly fascinating book-object when it simply starts and ends with no attention paid to the strangeness of holding this accretion of cotton and tree and ink that's carried through the centuries as some potentially holy writ—the dissembling of Sartre's *Roquentin*, breaking down the elements of life in *Nausea*, elucidates the large and the small dimensions of the sentence, the book, and though it can lead to madness, *to* dissembling, it can also lead to fuller life, to wonder. As writers we need to pursue that, the new, and part of that is and has to be reconceiving of written entities so that our readers might reconceive of them — in turn reconceiving of language; think for instance of the words that did not exist pre-Shakespeare — pushing things onward and outward so that our readers are able to experience that newness not just of the book or the text, but of ourselves, our interior language, applied to that book or text.

I don't know that I think it's possible to reconcile the individual with society, and I think you could possibly draw an accurate illustration of the history of mankind based upon the failures of this premise. I don't know, not for sure. If I look at my own life there does seem to be this discrepancy between who I view myself to be, and how this might not align with the society in which I find myself positioned. I say that's fine, and writing, it's certainly fine. If you can position yourself this way, and treat your language as individual at every turn, resisting the temptation to affix it to something apparently stabler — but not innate to you — the process will bring about sentences that *are* individual, that you can choose to implant in paragraphs or leave on their own, that's not my concern, far more so it's about trusting in the individuating impulse each person has, of asserting who they are, of risking the horror of being who they are, and fighting that fight, and the work should reflect this, and it's worth it to pull your sentences from their ideal differentiated state to then find their context in the work, and to revise this, and to apportion it then to the thing that will go out into the world of people.

When you're devoting time and attention to the way your mind forms sentences and makes associations, you're putting something out there that truly doesn't and can't exist anywhere else, and thus the cultivation of your own types of sentences should be as willfully subjective as you're able to manage, as it will save you time spent wondering if you're missing something, and abiding by the senses of people you've deemed authorities in this practice. I don't have or want any authority. I don't seek authority. I'm just seeking sentences. The sentences of novelizations of B-movies from the 1970s, the sentences of manuals, of assignments, of DeLillo, of *whatever*. I want it all. Opening oneself to these things in both our own work and our own serious reading of these resonant things allows for entry of sentences from the whole of life, from conversations with your parents, your boss, your daughter, and opens one to the artfulness in the whole of life, which for its intermingling with the human spirit, becomes and remains the

writer's surest source of sustenance, and
the terrain in which you'll be able to
put your sense of things to the world.

COMPO-

AS

-TION

-SITION

EXPLANA-

"Composition as Explanation" Stein, Gertrude
https://www.poetryfoundation.org/articles/69481/composition-as-explanation

There is singularly nothing that makes a difference a difference in beginning and in the middle and in ending except that each generation has something different at which they are all looking. By this I mean so simply that anybody knows it that composition is the difference which makes each and all of them then different from other generations and this is what makes everything different otherwise they are all alike and everybody knows it because everybody says it.

In trying to approach Stein's manifesto—first delivered as a lecture — I'm tempted to simply copy and paste the entire thing and let that suffice for this section of the book. The wonderful thing about Stein is she is so singularly *herself* in all of her writing, such that to try and summarize, or comment upon it, brings a simultaneous awe and admiration that's rather stupefying—Sianne Ngai calls it "stuplimity" in her magnificent *Ugly Feelings* — and it's difficult to even go about discussing Stein because of this feeling. There's a desire to let her take the reins. If you were to get together with a friend after you'd both read *The Making of Americans*, I'd imagine most of the conversation would be about *the feeling* of reading the work, rather than its actual content. Nevertheless, because I do consider myself not only a fan of Stein, but an adherent to what I've gleaned from her approach, I want to try and engage frankly with "Composition as Explanation," to see where it goes.

I think there's something special in her use of the word "difference," or the idea of difference, that has a lot in common with certain ideas of Gilles Deleuze, sometimes referred to as the philosopher of difference. Here, and in Deleuze, difference is often treated as a way of reading or interpreting the world, of reading and interpreting texts, because at root we understand what something is by comparing it to whatever it isn't, and this is the case especially in language, in words, which are discernible not only by their characters, and sounds, but by their surrounding context — which overlaps with Lutz' thinking—and the pairings and makeup we've grown used to digesting in our language for its messages as we move throughout a written work. Stein wasn't presenting "Composition as Explanation" as a grammarian, nor as a college English professor. These were talks given that were guided and infused by her own work, and her own approach to what would become known as the Modernist project, to varied literary clubs at Cambridge and at Oxford — a version was published, too, by Hogarth Press; and of course it has gone on to be reissued. It was set up by Edith Sitwell, who was also one of the first people to develop and sustain an interest in the works of James Purdy. I mention Purdy because I think it fits to read him through the lens of Stein's ideas, and I especially mention Sitwell because she was a kind of Stein figure for Purdy, and other artists in a range of artforms, hosting salons and the like wherein people could share work, discuss their ideas.

Stein's ability to take relatively common terms and reiterate them with a renewed energy feels impossible to really replicate. It's the key distinction between a massive contemporaneous literary endeavor like Proust's, or Joyce's, and Stein's, who in comparison reads as though she's dead set on a simple language, but with that language she is going to extract every possible morsel of feeling. Because of her language and her use of it, reading Stein can feel as though you're encountering an English that's entirely other, something almost alien. The equally fascinating thing is I could say exactly that about *Finnegans Wake*, but I would be talking about something totally different.

It is very likely that nearly every one has been very nearly certain that something that is interesting is interesting them. Can they and do they. It is very interesting that nothing inside in them, that is when you consider the very long history of how every one ever acted or has felt, it is very interesting that nothing inside in them in all of them makes it connectedly different. By this I mean this. The only thing that is different from one time to another is what is seen and what is seen depends upon how everybody is doing everything.

(Ibid., second paragraph)

I think there's sort of an aggressive
note in saying these things very exactly, even though they often appear to
veer off into the nonsensical—*almost*—because that determination of what she's
saying makes the experience of taking it in
feel artful, assured. I say aggressive but
in any recordings I've heard of Stein she
appears incredibly calm. There's a lulling
rhythm we might get from a Steven Wright
performance, or a longer stretch of Albert
Ayler's music. The language can feel rushed,
energized, but there's also that assured-
ness. *By this I mean this* — it's such a
beautiful sentence. And this really is
the thing each writer can be given when
they begin to assemble themselves in their
work, the notion that they are permitted to commune with the language however
they see fit, however they *need* to, and
this is Stein finding a way to actually
say and demonstrate this to an audience.

Nothing changes from generation to gen-eration except the thing seen and that makes a composition. (Ibid., cont'd)

There is nothing to say excepting every single thing in every possible manner in which something might be said. There is nothing to consider excepting every disparity between every single thing and to try to put it down rightly. In writing her history of a family she tried to write the history of all families, in writing about how she writes anything she tries to write about all who might wind up writing something and figuring out what they need to figure out. She's not trying to simplify what she's talking about to its bare elements, she's trying to *convey* the simplifying of what she's talking about through the speech act, and in the process to make it digestible not just as text, or as lecture, but as this hybrid of performing her ideas in the language she's come to view as her own, as her way of looking at the world and trying to make a composition from that looking. So what is seen is what changes, the things of the world are changed. Plastic takes over. Television takes over. All things die. Wars go on. These are the things which differentiate writers and what they will see and how they will see it. People persist in their peopledom, their peoplehood, and these things are the things that make up their compositions—how do you see? — their renderings of living and of experience for people to encounter, all people. This is the composition, the practice, the process, of looking at the world and trying to satisfactorily render that looking, that seeing. This is a moment in the world where certainty isn't around, where-artists are dealing with things heaped at their feet, and relentless disease, and fighting, and poverty, and political insanity, this is our inheritance and it is the same as it was for Stein as it is now, here, now, it just *looks* different. This is an attempt to craft a mode of writing out of that state and it seems an impossibility, so the method of necessity becomes this slow manipulating of the words she's using until they're put right.

This makes the thing we are looking at very different and this makes what those who describe it make of it, it makes a composition, it confuses, it shows, it is, it looks, it likes it as it is, and this makes what is seen as it is seen. Nothing changes from generation to generation except the thing seen and that makes a composition. (Ibid.)

Stein is trying to articulate what a work of art would even be, what a composition would even be, and when it becomes whatever it is, not being the process of its making any longer but its final composition state. It is finished. First is this notion of difference, then beauty, and then there's this sort of murky space where something is taken in as a *classic* or is not, and if something is taken in as a *classic* it can become sort of tepid, or lose its luster. This is something everyone knows. She also highlights the timeline of things which art can change, which is possibly less apparent here, now, but talking at the beginning of the twentieth century, after one-hundred-plus years of what's really a relative consistency in terms of what writing did and was expected to do — and certainly in terms of the "classic," and what would've been considered classic both when Stein delivered this and one hundred years before this — it is interesting to think about how jarring it might've been to see work published that way with so many extant kind of entrenched ideas or assumptions about literature or art. Stein is this mediator then, between versions of the written word that were in some ways difficult to reconcile.

Each period of living differs from any other period of living not in the way life is but in the way life is conducted and that authentically speaking is composition. After life has been conducted in a certain way everybody knows it but nobody knows it, little by little, nobody knows it as long as nobody knows it. Any one creating the composition in the arts does not know it either, they are conducting life and that makes their composition what it is, it makes their work compose as it does. (Ibid.)

Artists try to respond to the vicissitudes of history with something apt to the task, and the movement of industry brought about all kinds of questions about what the world would even be in one year's time, not to mention ten or twenty — this is the world we have inherited too. Stein, then, is giving an accounting of what she's observed in those salons, in her world, her reading, her looking, not just in terms of their writing, but the visual art and the music they created as well. It's an impossible task, which I think accounts for her approach being what it is — it's also an impossible task to write the history of all families, which accounts for the form *The Making of Americans* takes. Here is a unique case wherein the language of a kind of manifesto meets the form and content of the things it advocates in art — the form is the content, the content the form. By inserting herself, her method, her ideas in this moment, Stein is taking some of the burden onto herself, and her response to this burden is to immerse herself in this approach to sentence-making, to making her art, and in certain terms to let this speak for itself — *By this I mean this.*

No one thinks these things when they are making when they are creating what is the composition, naturally no one thinks, that is no one formulates until what is to be formulated has been made. *(Ibid.)*

161

Stein, through whatever, seems always to have been thoroughly herself, so that even here, when she has this opportunity to potentially direct interest toward her work, to perhaps render accessible the natures of her works that are less than accessible, she explains how she composes *how she composes*. Whether there's any dimension of her work that might be called a "bit," she seldom, if ever, lets any mask slip; she has found her language, her relationship to her language, so she needn't waver. Stein is always immensely serious and hilarious, writing *as* spoken in a rambled spree of thought. Here I see notes of that state previously mentioned, entering a kind of willed, not ignorance, but quiet, the brain being quieted down because the brain is needed only to assemble the results once they've been put, or *formulated*, per Stein.

As writers, we need to be able to balance the pure expressive state we can enter into if we get into the habit of sitting down and taking something seriously. Some need to write standing, stark naked, for this. Some need to write at dawn, quiet, with coffee, or tea. Some need a laptop, in bed, simple. Some need a pencil, a particular pencil, *this* pencil. You'll try out as many of these approaches as is needed before you find the thing that's the surest things for you, and even then it might change after several compositions, stories, novels, novellas, essays. It's always moving, and we are always following. We also get hints at the editing process, the revision process, even simply the willingness to remain with it and return to it and pursue it. On the one hand we want to reach this state of pure expression, often the rambling, logorrheic thing can be most effective here; however we also need to be thinking of that end formulation, and how we'll want it put. Is what we're writing becoming a story, a novel, a lecture? What are the conditions under which these things come to exist, and how can my sentences fit within that larger context — again, it helps to think here of the individual in relation to the larger society, *oppose things*, be they structures, stories, whatever — so that the thing can finally be completed for our purposes.

After that I did a book called
The Making of Americans it is a long
book about a thousand pages.

Here again it was all so natural to me
and more and more complicatedly a con-
tinuous present. A continuous present
is a continuous present. I made almost a
thousand pages of a continuous present.
(Ibid.)

This notion of the "continuous present" is useful in formulating this ideal mindset in which you're able to generate sentences that align with your desires for them, always being there, being present, living in the real context of your sentence. As with meditation, prayer, the writer can divorce themselves from time as such, and transcribe information that enters there in the same way a person can understand typically quieted parts of themselves through a sustained process of sitting, quietly. A continuous present, for a writer, either the reality of the thing in which we're working, the story, the piece, or the mindset we're working to enter into when the work seems to be going quite well. Often it can feel like transcription, a voice from some other place, but within — the world inside the world. Recursion, too, a return, toward the thing we've just left, upon the words we've just written down. We begin, and we begin again, and in the process we return, and we return again, to our subject, to our scene, to our narrative, all by way of the sentence we find ourselves occupying, only there, needing to make our way out— through — much like the ouroboran sentences of Delany or of Joyce. Remaining with that thing that's troubling you, remaining with the words as they're coming out, and not being afraid to push, to force something through, to push and to push and to push with the will through the writing of the sentence that will give way to the language you then need to arrive at, in that continuous present of the thing, at the present moment, working through.

So it is not easy, no. It forces you to think differently about how words can work. Stein's work and ideas are best taken in slowly, and I'm tempted to say ambiently — please do listen to her reading from *The Making of Americans*, several times— as if they're given in *this* voice, the lecturer's voice, and perhaps we tune in and out, not because what she's saying doesn't seem important, but because it's being delivered honestly, without hyperbole, like conversation, honest, considered conversation, much in the way her books are fairly unadorned, without frenzied highs except for in these bare words. Even *Tender Buttons*, which might be Stein's most exuberant text, it offers a reading experience that's a wonderful lulling along.

There is at present there is distribution, by this I mean expression and time, and in this way at present composition is time that is the reason that at present the time-sense is troubling that is the reason why at present the time-sense in the composition is the composition that is making what there is in composition. (*Ibid.*)

Yes, the redundancy, yes, the repetitiveness, and the embrace at times of apparent nonsense — I think these are part and parcel with *all* of Stein. We have to remember the figure of Stein in her rooms, talking with painters and composers and drunks and writers and celebrities and actors, and holding their interest and their attention long enough not only to entertain them, but to command a presence that proved undeniable in all the lives she touched. There's a kind of Andy Kaufman register she reaches that I think fits, but Stein wasn't some wild individual plucked from the shadows and given a pen and paper, she was highly educated and engaged with art and thought for the majority of her life, hungrily. I think multiplicity, returning, continued engagement, were concerns of Stein's, and the notion of offering something that grows, that compounds somehow, goes through permutations, seems absolutely in line with someone so concerned with industrialization, and repetition.

Possibly it's useful to think of compositions as "objects" in this context, in the way I referred to thinking about sentences as objects. Stein has excelled — especially in *Tender Buttons* — at taking one object and extrapolating immediately to the nth degree both in abstract, poetic phrasing, and in unanticipated associative thinking — again, too, the writing as psychoanalytic free association. This, and her relationship with words — being objects — seems to clarify a reading of her ideas *on* writing to some degree. Composition was an act for her, situated in time, and affected not only by one's moment but by the moments of one's influences and the moments of all those experiencing this same thing, potentially seeing it differently. Composition, accordingly, was complicated, confounding, but the only recourse for Stein was to turn one's approach inward, letting composition thusly become quite literally an explanation of one's feelings on a topic, a story, a time, a sight, whatever it is, and doing so in the continuous present as much as possible to keep the thing freshly there in front of your eyes, open to its movements and informed by your perception — what you "see" — at every moment in making the wording that will then account for whatever it is you're witnessing.

There is at present there is distribution, by this I mean expression and time, and in this way at present composition is time that is the reason that at present the time-sense is troubling that is the reason why at present the time-sense in the composition is the composition that is making what there is in composition.

And afterwards.

Now that is all.

(Ibid.)

SENTIENCE:

DEATH

MEMOIRING

But this is the rule, and there is no way to free oneself of it: as soon as the thought has arisen, it must be followed to the very end.

Maurice Blanchot

The Son of God was born an outcast, in order to tell us that every outcast is a child of God. He came into the world as each child comes into the world, weak and vulnerable, so that we can learn to accept our weaknesses with tender love.

@pontifex

It became popular for people to pluck and assemble in such a way that every new book announced seemed tethered to these ideas of genre-blurring, opening and associating and the like. Someone somewhere said something was not quite a novel, nor a biography, nor a scientific treatise. I hear this sort of thing and I think that that means it is a novel. The second something becomes unwieldy but in an ideal sense, and we're not certain who is speaking, and we don't quite understand what we're encountering, it would appear to me to be a novel. It could be any thing, though. And naming is a dumb thing. We were on the rocks by the river in Lewiston, Idaho recently. I picked up a rock that was gorgeous and pink. It looked like a marbled, uncooked steak. I held it and I thought about the one class I'd taken on rocks and the things I barely remembered. I didn't know the name for this rock. I thought, well, I could name it. Someone, at some point, named this rock. In the Latin. Someone named this rock in the Latin, and enough people agreed, and thus it was so. I wanted to name this rock. I wanted to simply name this rock something, but then I realized I would have to then kneel down and occupy myself with naming every other rock there on the beach of rocks. And a man was fly-fishing. And my children were looking around. And we had this bag of rocks. I thought that might be a worthwhile fictive endeavor, to start with something, and to name it, and to then have to name every other thing because I'd pulled the thread, and it was time to name the rest of the things in the world. An Estimated 50 Billion Birds Populate Earth, but Four Species Reign Supreme. Neanderthals Cooked Surprisingly Complex Meals. China Launches Three Astronauts to Its Space Station. And so is this lying? Is this the act of lying? Is the naming of things lying? Putting something down is this lying? Naming birds is this lying? Writing a memoir made of rot is this lying? Burying your intention somewhere in what someone else is saying, is this lying?

I   do   not   read.

I can remember when I used to live in Chicago and I tried to read as much of everything as I could, always, always reading, looking. My first fall there I remember reading Kenneth Clark's *The Nude on the El* as I made my way downtown for classes, or home for the late nights, the writing, the TV, the painting, the books. The mass market paperback, and poring over the images, the text, attempting to understand something, compelled by something, living.

I believe I come from a time when fathers believed they ought to act in a sort of way that was contingent with their fathers, and their fathers were removed, and so my father was sort of removed, and I don't understand who he was, and I try to understand who he was, but the more I try to understand it the more cloudy the picture becomes, and I'm not trying to be dramatic because that's really how it is, and I'm not trying to tell anybody how they ought to be but this is my situation. We are seeking our fathers in perpetuity. My father's life was cut short too quickly. There are worlds within this world. I don't have any idea what a person ought to do. The Minnesota Multiphasic Personality Inventory is a thing given to people to understand the categories in which they might fit in terms of various risks and indicators as to which modes of treatment might be most effective. It's like an exam. I don't remember what it told me about my father. I know I talked to my father about taking it. I don't know how I did on the exam. I don't know how so many questions could indicate anything about any person at all. My father was a good man.

I think that lying is one of the only constants in life.

When I am with my wife, and we are in the kitchen, and the day is either mostly done or we are feeling as though a hardship has been passed, there will sometimes come a joke, or some comment on my nature—as it is a pathetic nature — and on the best days this is something deeply nourishing; I can feel life being pumped back into my chest. Often, though, I — as it is a pathetic nature—behave like a child.

I think it was in my second fall that I first tried to read Deleuze and Guattari. I think I got it the Christmas before, and brought it to Chicago with me, and I left my apartment in Rogers Park—I lived alone then — before heading downtown where I was taking an evening course focused on fiction writing and censorship. When you're young and figuring things out there's something special about a class at night. Walking around at night, crazed, feeling closer to what you're reading about, feeling alive. You put your hands in your pockets, you slug some coffee wherever you can get it, you ride elevators and walk down long hallways. It's perfect.

This was my second time taking that particular class, as I'd stopped attending classes two or three weeks before the end of the spring semester the year previous, intending on doing something other than go back to school in Chicago; but really just getting terribly, terribly depressed, staying up all night, walking around the city, obsessive. Saying words whose definitions I didn't know over and over, with their definitions, trying to control it, to remember them, to be smarter, a better writer. Repeating, over and over and over again.

I tried to write something like *The Tunnel*
once. I hadn't finished reading *The Tunnel*
when I'd done it. This is a situation with
which I'm not unfamiliar. The first Winter of my married life. I am not Kohler,
though, or Gass. I don't have that in me,
I don't think. I don't have much in me, if
I'm honest. I'm not much, as it turns out,
as a person. We got married in the Winter. They say not to capitalize seasons.
We got married in the Winter. I don't
know what my life is like. I don't have
a comparison to make or a grand observation to share. I feel married. I live in
the world as a person within a marriage.
I don't know what this means, however. We
don't have a lot of money. Growing up we
had money, sure. We're not broke compared
to some, sure. Still, though, we don't
have a lot of money. I don't get paid
well for my work, not this work or the
other work. I don't know if I ever will.
We have not lived the right kind of life.

This would've meant the class was in spring the first year, and fall the second, but I can't swear to that. I received the nice Penguin Classics edition of *Anti-Oedipus*, and I think I was 120 or so pages into it when I rode the train downtown and I sat reading it while smelling the piss that was there on the El. I miss that piss smell still. I went to class, and it might've been the time when I asked the teacher what else he did besides teaching. I thought at the time that he only taught that class, and knew he was a published writer, so I think I asked just trying to understand more about this guy I admired. He, and other students, took it to be me sizing him up, trying to appear smarter, or more active, or something. If they knew how I spent my days I can only trust they would've understood this was not my intention, but whatever. I think it was that day because I felt this need to do something to sort of remove me from the situation and thus what I did with the book. Maybe, or maybe not, I'm just not sure.

I don't know how other people in the world perceive me. I know that sometimes it seems like I'm doing well socially, but this is consistently followed by the sense that I am a kind of leper, that I smell, that I'm obnoxious, that I'm going to be found out.

I'd gone there for school. I first went when I was nineteen. I don't know if I was happy but I loved Chicago. Most of my life I have struggled with a combination of mental disorders, and struggled to balance out the treatment of these things with my life. I would go off meds, and read a lot, but be intensely obsessive and suicidal all the while. Or I'd go to therapy as much as I could, and take the medicine, but I'd start to second-guess things and spend my time thinking something else was terribly wrong. I first went to Chicago when I was taking Effexor for the first time, when I was nineteen. That was one of few life-changing experiences I've ever had with medication. I felt fundamentally grateful to be alive, and very enthused by life, most days. Then, and I don't remember the motivation, I flushed my meds. That was the first year. I don't know what medications I took or did not take my second year. I know I drank a lot of non-alcoholic beer and a *lot* of coffee. I've heard of people trying to drink 30 or 40 NA beers while trying to remain "sober," or expressing their desire to remain clean. I never did anything like that, but it was certainly tiptoeing close to relapse, amidst everything else. It was a bad time, in many respects. If I feel any fondness now it is for the city, its movie theaters, the El, and certain moments writing, reading books, or watching films and having coffee.

I haven't yet read Christopher Lasch, and I don't know that I will. I haven't read much Paglia. I think Michel Houellebecq is overrated, and I've never actually seen someone discussing his work—they discuss the person, and that's about the extent of it. I don't know if freedom in this regard is something to be sought. Sexual freedom. Libertinage. I think the world is fundamentally an impossible colliding of humanity's impossibility, and I don't think a person has a right to indicate anything about the freedoms of another. We don't need freedom.

The bathroom on the third floor of the building where this class was held had this window that opened into this spot where four buildings met, but there wasn't enough room to do anything with it, so what remained was this impossible space between these structures. I loved to go in there and to open it and to look outside into it. In my memory there's a roof above it, that made it glow a hazy blue, awkward edges of these four compressed buildings, with nothing useable for whoever owned each one.

I tend to romanticize my time in Chicago in retrospect, but the majority of the time that I was there, and anywhere, really, I was pretty miserable — people are often asking my wife if I'm particularly affected by a situation, a meeting, say, or an appointment. "No," she'll often say, "that's just how his face looks…" Without really intending to, I look like a miserable person. I think I feel less miserable now, having kids, having a family, a career, but I still look it. That was a point in my life when I felt disconnected from most everything. I was unhappy, and I was obsessive — and undiagnosed as having OCD, as the kind of OCD I have, "harm OCD," is an odd thing to pin down when depression and anxiety and the like are already on the table. I did strange things to try and feel content, or like I was pushing back — *oppose things*. Of course I thought about jumping down into the space between the buildings, outside of the window. Down below it looked like there weren't openings — I saw windows, but they were industrial, like they wouldn't open at all — so as I leaned out I imagined jumping out and breaking my legs, and being stuck down there until someone like me opened one of the upper windows and looked down, or heard me scream out.

I can only speak to my own experience with the library and it has been a wonderful experience although it has also collided miserably with my addictive self which has resulted in no shortage of stupidity. I have books right now that I got mailed from the library at my university that I have more or less forgotten about. Raymond Federman's books. Some others. An Elmore Leonard compendium. I don't know whether I'm a terrible nuisance to these people. I almost said terrific nuisance. Perhaps terrific nuisance is just fine. I think I probably am. Most places I've been there has inevitably been some thing which went unreturned. And they told me. And I complained. And I tried to tell them I'd returned it all. And they said I didn't. And I didn't. And so it went and went. Once it was a DVD of the film version of *The Talented Mr. Ripley*, and I didn't watch it. I went through this long ordeal and eventually contacted another library, the local public library where I was living in Eau Claire, Wisconsin, to ask them whether a DVD I'd returned there had contained this DVD and if I could exchange the discs. I ordered a new copy from Amazon. I gave the new copy to the library where I'd returned an empty box. The public library said they had no idea. I returned the DVD and weeks later opened a DVD player at my father's house and found it. Then more recently it was a book called *The Work of Fire*, by Maurice Blanchot, and I never read it.

I accidentally dropped it off at a donation bin at a Hope center and then received an email about the book needing to be returned at my university library. I think I've talked about this somewhere else. I called the Hope center and went in there several times to dig through this massive bin. I lied and told the library that I swore I'd returned it. They were kind. I hate myself. Nothing happened. I'd enjoy that kind of work. I enjoy working with people I know are lying. That's not true.

I stopped taking Seroquel and Fluvoxamine and since then I haven't had the twitches I typically had on both of those medications — today I've just eaten a great deal after having caffeine and now I'm watching something on the internet; I never liked being on Seroquel — I'm waiting now to hear back about my GeneSight test.

So these things transpired, my life transpired, in varying order, but what was important was this feeling of a connection to this book, Deleuze and Guattari, alongside this feeling of a sort of childish anger, a desire to spit on or at something, both metaphorically and otherwise. This would've been the only retort I'd have had mentally against the things I felt, this dumb desire to jump out of a window or walk into traffic. I think there can be a purity to that youthful kind of anger, and I remember feeling it about being in school at that point, and feeling as though I was wasting my time, my life, that I'd never bring anything to materialize with all the writing, and submitting, and failing I did. This might be the danger of my thinking about writing then. My understanding was based on feelings. I loved reading Frederick Exley because it felt so special, alive, angry, miserable, but purposeful in that misery. I loved watching things like *Taxi Driver* for the same reason, or Pasolini films. I loved these things because they made me feel something, whatever it might've been. I wrote, then, because of that feeling, my feelings. I thought if I wrote when angry it could let someone feel that. I pursued it, then. I pursued *only* it, most of my days. Either that or I was shut off. So I wanted this book, by these apparently angry writers, pushing back against orthodoxy in their fields. I sought the expression of the thing, a feeling, something, a reality, a *friend*. Perhaps I felt it, and didn't, as I did with every aesthetic

experience, every thing. So if it isn't
offered, or if I simply felt some other
thing, then fuck it, and I could turn.

My father used to ask me about my diabetes, whether I just didn't care, whether it was a sort of nihilism, but I think that's putting it too romantically. The truth is that I am incredibly lazy, incredibly incredibly lazy, and I think I'm a glutton, and these two things often get entwined and the result can be a person like me, a person who lives like this.

Whatever happened, here's what happened:
I went to class, and I was fed up, and
I did dumb shit in class, and then when
class was done, and it was late, I went
outside into the Chicago night — that
glorious thing — and I felt angry, *mad*,
so I started to walk toward the lake—and
I think I wrote this somewhere before—
and I kept walking, walking, and I was
reading from the book under the street-
lights, and I went on and on until I got
to the water, and I held the book in my
right hand, and I whipped it like a flat
stone over the water... and I felt so much
better, and I knelt down there next to
the water — *did I do this? did I really kneel there and do this?* — and I
calmed myself down a bit and I realized what
I had done, and I went to the train station,
and I got on the train and I took it home —
quieted, quieted — and I don't know who I
would've talked to, and I don't know if I
smoked any cigarettes, and I don't know if
I ate chips, or went to the grocery store,
or stayed up all night watching *Cheers*,
or what I did; but there was energy. I'm
always throwing meaningful shit
away. I don't know what it means.
I quit a lot. I *like* to quit — is
that it? Dumb youthful nihilism, hm. Thinking about that time I'm 60% of a person, if
that. My bare room, my shitty TV set. My
bathroom, the closet there was pretty big.
Every relationship. People all around.
Threats all around. Slices of pizza. Dumb
juvenile graffiti. I'm *twenty-one*. I don't
know if I went to *one* AA meeting in Chicago,
in fact I know I didn't—does that matter?

There is a notion of autobiography that I sometimes feel tethered to, and then I look at the world, and my thinking goes quiet, and I know precisely when I'll be dead. Everything is put off, and should be put off, as most things can be reliably put off until you're dead. I first took the MMPI when I was fifteen years old. Maybe I'd taken it before that. I've only ever been hospitalized in the state of Minnesota.

For much of my life I was what I think of as a sort of artless person. Even now. When an addict or alcoholic is in active addiction their focus tends to allow itself to become pretty fixated; the sharpness of the world is quieted by this fixation, the ugly reality of the morning is fuzzed-over. I first started to drink and to use drugs with a relative consistency when I was eleven, and used thereafter until finally sobering up at seventeen. For at least those six years my interests—in addition to the usual sexual experimentation, music, and what friendships I did have — left little room for art, in any capacity, and whatever else, no school, nothing. I wasn't on heroin or anything, but I was at least mostly sort of vaguely fucked-up on whatever substances I could access, either through friendship, stealing, money, or trade — I'd steal a handful of speed and trade it with a friend for some booze or something, a night. I used to have a sort of pride that I didn't read, or hadn't read much. I used to say I would die by twenty-one. I'm type one diabetic and at the rate I used and drank—commingled with really no attention paid to blood sugars and the like, though I did consistently take my insulin at night and for each meal; and if I was pissing a lot, or clearly the kind of mad a high blood sugar will make you — it really wasn't an outlandish idea that I'd only be around for ten years or so. That was my mindset, and I was fine with it. I didn't really know what to do with life, with the world.

I guess I did see films, though, and I've always watched a lot of television. I was introduced to some good music during this period, but literature or art were basically nothing to me, and that really didn't matter to me at all.

I have problems with my irritability, and often I'll be sitting, angry, at most everyone around me, and I'll realize it's over nothing, and often then I'll find my bloodsugar is high, or something equally stupid and medical. I heard once that if you hate everyone, eat something; and if you think everyone hates you, go to bed. I think it's true.

By now most people know about Glenn Gould's tendency to run progressively hotter water over his hands before performances. I don't think it's just about the water however. There's something essential about the contemporary human animal standing at the sink and dealing with something, and there's something equally essential about giving yourself over to this experience, hunching over and leaning your elbows on the edges of the sink and letting the water run. When I feel something I often feel it in the coldness of my hands or feet first. I've taken to sometimes wearing two pairs of socks when I'm doing something anxiety-inducing, or sometimes wearing fingerless gloves when doing various tasks because it seems more acceptable than wearing gloves or mittens with full covering inside. My father had this same affliction. He took beta blockers before piano recitals because of it. Once after I'd gotten sober I took a couple the day before I was supposed to work at a telemarketing job. I consider this a slip.

Stuff began to change the first time I went to rehab, at fifteen. Whether you're turning to literature for something then, or something else, the beginning of the traditional recovery process involved a good deal of reading, writing, talking, and listening. A friend sent me *To a God Unknown* by John Steinbeck. I don't think I read it for two years or so, but the idea that it was nice to have books around you did begin to set in, and I grew to like the process of reading and writing. I wrote and read on the computer before rehab, but in my head it's a different thing. The idea of writing, of art, or any of that didn't get solidified until the second time I was in treatment, going in at sixteen, and turning seventeen while there. I now see that if I'd been smarter with money as an addict, or gone to certain places rather than others, I don't think I'd have survived that year between my time in treatment. I struggle with the idea of addiction sometimes. I struggle with AA and that kind of thing being the only solution. When I think, though, about the time between my time in treatment, it becomes pretty clear. The lying, the insatiable appetite for literally anything numbing, it got to be pretty clear that I needed to figure things out.

When I lived alone in Minnesota I used to spend a lot of time walking around or sitting in my apartment watching TV on my computer and it got to feeling like I was actively rotting my existence into a state of non-being, or like I was steadily eroding my living into a place of real inward discomfort. I was angry, but I was also terribly lonely, and I was trying to find my place in the world and coming up with nothing at all. Because of this I'd enter into relationships, and leave, and push people away, and hurt people, and it would make the whole process progressively more complicated, as I got more miserable, and more uncomfortable, with less and less of a sense that there was something I could do. I remember feeling real fear, walking around, and the only context that seemed to give me peace or a sense of perspective was the claasroom, where I'd then hide for the following eight years. And I know about evil, and wrong, and I know that they are always right next to you.

Suddenly writing became important to me, in there, as did reading, and I started to develop this sense of myself as a person who wrote, who took writing seriously, and then someone who read, and who cared about art, in my then limited capacity of what that might even mean. I remember bringing around notebooks, books, pieces of paper I'd write things on. There was this sense, in treatment, of an unmanageability, which, of course there was. This sense, though, brought with it a searching for elements of my own life I might hold to, and one of those things was writing, and this was always in communication with what I was taking in, too. Reading, thinking back to music I felt connected to, writing down thoughts at an AA meeting in Minnesota, writing down stuff for step work in my halfway house. It appeared that a control offered itself there, so that even writing "I hate my life," or "I've fucked everything up so badly," felt better than to say it, because I could see it, I could expand upon it, it was *there*. I think this has made my relationship to literature and to art kind of difficult to articulate and to personally understand because it came from this really bizarre moment in my life. I came to need writing and art at a time in my life when I couldn't have felt more alienated. When I returned home, to high school, to real life, all the kids my age were just starting to get into drinking, or using milder drugs, with any frequency. I felt alone, and writing, I think, was something reliable that I could turn to. The alienation also consisted into my recovery. I moved from Minnesota — "the land of ten thousand treatment centers," where younger sober people were at most every meeting — to Eau Claire, Wisconsin, where the vast majority of people who were in recovery were twenty or thirty years older than me, at a minimum. I had a sense when I was in treatment that the approach to recovery that they were advocating—twelve steps, AA, NA, nothing else — might not entirely fit for the whole of my life, so I think I opened myself up to aspects of living that might guide me, and the notion of art, of writing, was perhaps the biggest.

I don't know what to do about attention.
Because on the one hand everything is incredibly interesting constantly, and on the
other. I'm a person with a life and with a
family and with a marriage and with a job
and with a car and with a phone and with a
mother and with my siblings and my nieces
and an entire world, and I worry about if
I sounded cool in a text message I sent.

I always struggle with a sense of the utility of art, because for me it's always felt one-sided — a writer writes something because they feel fucked up and need to give that a context — so it's difficult for me to say what experimental writing is "for". At the best times, it doesn't matter, and I don't think about it, I'm just working on projects. I think it's so loaded because I needed it so vitally when I first encountered it, so I want the purpose to align with that feeling of kind of being lost, but finding some salvation. I still feel as though I fundamentally need it, need to continue working — I don't write for money, and projects are only completed if there's a feeling like I need to do them — but the other side of it is always strange to me. All this talk about the death and the life of novels, of film, of art. I'm as susceptible to it as anybody, I guess. I go around in want of a concrete answer, something definitive.

I used to close my eyes when I drove if I was the only person on the road, and I used to steal, and I used to spraypaint graffiti, and I used to hurt myself, and I used to sleep with the wrong people, and I used to talk to the wrong people, and I used to take anything, and I once took Foxgloves immediately after my father had told me they were poisonous, and I once ate pennies, and I used to walk around late into the night in Chicago, sneering and violent, and I used to pick fights, and I used to make threats, and I used to court every pathetic kind of misery, and I used to flush my meds, and I used to spend recklessly on anything, and I used to eat anything, and I used to drink anything, and I used to drop out of everything, and I used to ride the train anywhere, and I used to think about hanging myself all day, every day, and I used to think about shooting myself, and I used to want to cut off my finger — I went through all these steps to explain how I'd cut off my finger — but I never did it.

I was younger, and fresh out of rehab, and I knew that I wanted to continue writing. There was this feeling. I'd started in there, writing, talking about it, reading about it, trying to figure something out. My mother gave me a notebook, I think, and this treatment center had a computer. You could play solitaire or write, and they had a printer. I wrote this story about aliens, and alcoholics, and drug addicts, since I was surrounded by alcoholics and drug addicts. I knew that I was at a turning point wherefrom I would not be capable of living if I got back into drinking again, doing drugs again, and so I had to figure out things that I would do with my life now that I would not be dying before my twenty-first birthday. I read what I could in there. I know in my halfway house they had one of Arthur Janov's books in a shelf, facing a part of the living room we never went into, I kept it. Later on I really enjoyed reading about Primal Therapy, I watched videos about it and the connection that existed between Janov and Raphael Montañez Ortiz, who would do these performances where he'd set up a grand piano, and before an audience, would sometimes record, sometimes not, himself slowly destroying it with an axe. Four months into treatment I was given a recommendation of a halfway house, where I then went for around a month, maybe more, both of which were in Minnesota. I left, then, and I got to feeling like writing was the thing that certain people were maybe best-suited to do, and I had no idea whether someone like myself

— sort of an idiot but compelled nonetheless — could ever really write something worthwhile. I started reading more, and going to the public library a lot, and I ordered books online a lot, and I realized after reading certain things — the one that most stands out is *The Place of Dead Roads*, but also Hemingway's *Garden of Eden*, *American Psycho* and all of Ellis — I realized, slowly, that the practice of writing could take a lot of different shapes, and it appeared it could take a shape I felt I needed it to so it might work for me (largely an idiot).

When you're younger you think of your anger as a clarifying force, and you strip
away the minutia of living through it.
When you get older you hold onto aspects
of your anger, but life inevitably beats
some vulnerability out of you, and your
anger can start to feel pathetic, and the
longer you look at your despicable human
body in the mirror, the more pathetic you
feel, and the less angry you feel, and
the more you might desire to be crushed
under the boot of some invading army of
miserable giants. I still get too angry.

I think I view myself as potentially largely artless now, though I do feel determined to figure things out in terms of my
own writing, and this requires a level of
at least engaging with art, *trying*. I think
I did have a certain respect for language,
and I can remember moments when language
stood out, and I got captivated by it, but
so much of my dumb life until I was nineteen, twenty, probably even older was so
driven by this stupid animal inclination
that I don't know when one thing stopped,
and the other kind of took over, and I
became really determined to do something
with writing in my life. When I say artless I mean I watch a lot of videos on
YouTube. When I say artless I mean that
I don't dress particularly interestingly,
though I'm always seeing images of people
I'd like to look like. When I say artless
I mean that I don't talk about art every
day, though maybe that isn't true. When I
say artless I mean I think New York City
is overrated, so is LA, so is Portland.
When I say artless I mean I often struggle
to see any point of any of this, and in
turn I give over to the notion that there
might not be a point, and when I say artless I mean this makes me terribly, vul-
nerably bummed out. When I say artless I
mean I write a lot, but read relatively
little. When I say artless I mean I grew up
watching a lot of television, *a lot*. When
I say artless I mean I'm overweight, and on
Weight Watchers, no I'm intermittent fast-
ing, no I'm fat. When I say artless I mean I'm
not captivating, I'm too self-conscious to
be captivating, I'm not much of anything.

What could a person possibly do to enact anything they'd feel good about in any sense or capacity ever, please tell me.

My wife and I had met working at a camp for people with severe disabilities that summer before graduate school, and fallen in love, and driven together across the country at the end of it. The night we came in the hill was on fire as we descended the mountains from Montana and into the panhandle of Idaho. I wish I'd never gotten rid of the voicemail letting me know I'd been admitted to the program. The writer who left it is one of the kindest, most brilliant people I've ever met. She sounded as though she'd really read and enjoyed the stories I submitted — a piece called "Watertown Bodily" wherein I worshiped Frederick Exley, and a piece called "Pruitt-Igoe" wherein I worshiped Philip Glass and explored American ruins. She mentioned Dennis Cooper, who'd supported my writing, as he has so many writers, and she'd taught a seminar that semester including his work that I'd later learned proved mildly controversial. She'd loved his work and defended it, and her excitement about writing generally wasn't something I'd heard expressed aloud before. I'd finished undergrad late, the December before graduate school, when I was twenty-three, and I applied to four MFA programs. February went by with such anxiety. I thought I wouldn't get in anywhere. The first program I heard from said no. I don't know how much time went by.

I have an aversion to betting, to gam-
bling, I guess for the same reasons I have
an aversion to chess. I also think I have
an aversion to races, or games, because
excepting a slim few circumstances I really can't think of any time I've watched
either where I wasn't thinking I'd much
rather be doing just about anything else.
Baseball is nice, until it isn't. I really
can't get invested in watching people who
make more money in one year than I'll ever
make in my life do the things assholes used
to do when I was growing up. Forget it.

I really dislike particular films. I know of someone who works as a florist. I don't know whether they're happy or not. I know some-one whose mother was a florist, or worked in a flower shop. I don't know if I'd like it any more than anything I've ever done. I do like the anonymity of it, or the perceived anonymity of working with some-thing, and your presence having little to do with it except in the form of the work.

I don't know why other people come to feel like writing is the thing they need to do. I know that when it happens it's easy to feel like it might be a curse, a negative, but you need to remind yourself it's not, it's a gift. When I was younger I said that immortality was a reason I wanted to write. That sounds incredibly grandiose (stupid) in retrospect but the impulse was less about imposing myself on the consciousness of others and more about feeling terrified, truly scared, by the end of things. The notion of the universe dying, of the earth dying, and having done nothing that solidified my life, that gave shape to the thoughts I'd thought, the feelings I'd had. I didn't want to be famous, or even really known, I just wanted to put myself into these texts, these things that lived apart from me, and that would be enough. I can remember when I was freshly sober, I'd rent movies and I'd stay up late watching them, and at some point I'd text every single person in my phone something, just to feel engaged with these people I was drifting away from. They were partying, looking at schools, being young. I was getting obsessive, staying up, getting lost. It was sort of laughable and stupid, but the impulse gave way to the same impulse to have written something down that gets an ISBN, that at the very least might get stored digitally at the Library of Congress. I think when you're young, and basically alone, and without much in the way of responsibilities, and prone toward a sort of heavy depression, the notion of leaving something behind is quite important, much in the same way that remaining aware of your death is quite important. When I said things about immortality, I would in turn be hit with these thoughts of getting a suitcase, and filling it with all of these things I'd written, these scattered pages, and walking to the center of the city, and shooting myself in the head with a rifle. There's something to this way of thinking, or something common about this way of thinking, and I can see its ties with what I tried to write then and what I've tried to write thereafter. This simultaneous impulse toward a deathly gesture, and trying to put feeling into the work. If I could've opened up my brainstem, and touched it to a computer terminal, and published whatever got vomited out, it would've felt right.

I think it also speaks to a current interest I have in shorter books, both the writing of them and the reading of them. It's not just because we're all distracted, and our attention spans are shot, though that's certainly part of it. I look back, though, at the works of fiction that Blanchot published, and a work like *Nausea*, and there seems to be a sense within the shorter work, at least, of literature lending itself to a kind of performativity. Cesar Aira's approach to writing seems like the most sensible approach, unsentimental, utterly modern, but tied too to the impossible output of Georges Simenon or Donald E. Westlake. It's difficult, too, to be performative in a five-hundred-page novel, both for reader and writer alike.

You can't carry that register that long. Or you could, but it can start to feel like those night-long Andy Kaufman bits where he'd just read *The Great Gatsby* cover-to-cover. It's utterly compelling, and I would be in attendance, as I would gladly sit through a screening of Warhol's *Empire*, his eight hour film of a single shot of the Empire State Building, but the sort of effect I'm more interested in, which has to do with death, and has to do with language, and sentences working in such a way that they can hold a register for a sustained bit of relentless thought and reading. It's easier to reach in a short work, I guess, and I like the idea that I'm not, as a matter of course, asking more from readers than I'd really intend, not in terms of effort but in terms of length of effort. The notion, again, of Sianne Ngai's "stuplimity," I think, had an effect on me when I read it. Reading *The Making of Americans* had an effect on me when I read it, as did Darby Larson's *Irritant*. I like that effect, I've even loved that effect, that pronounced effect of an engaged sentence taking the shapes it seems to need to take; I've just come to prefer it in one-hundred pages rather than one-thousand, or even five-hundred.

I was suddenly reminded the other day of when I used to fill a cup with coffee, and grab two black tea bags, and put them in the coffee, and sit in the library at my undergraduate university to work and read. And then your life happens. And you see it peopled and rendered more complex. And you have grown more addicted to being entertained or distracted. And you see this affecting your ability to teach well. And you see it reflected in things students say in various places. And you want to be a good teacher which is incredibly difficult. And so you make a cup of tea and think about being younger, when there was an aggressiveness to pursuing things like knowledge or art, and maybe you do a better job or maybe you don't, but it won't be for lack of trying.

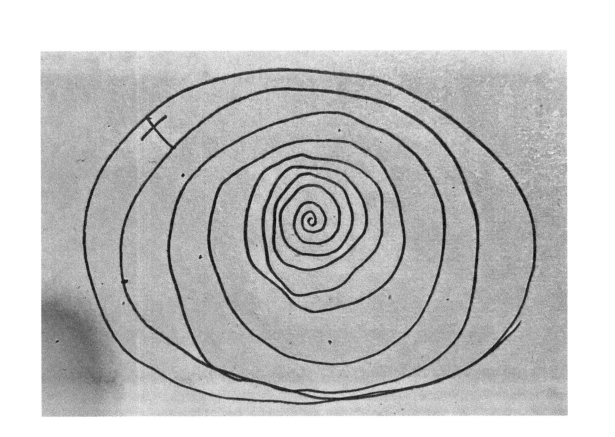

It's tempting to stop. It's tempting to resign yourself to a certain set of things. It's tempting to sit and spend all of your time doing one thing that informed the work, and gave you the work that felt most vital, but it's worth risking periods of a complete lack of vitality if in the process you're arriving at something that's more in tune with who you are at any particular moment in any particular corner of your life. I believe figures like Sartre and Gilles Deleuze were concerned with the primacy of language, of sentences, and thus their work has found such avid fans in writers.

Compelling thoughts, *human* thoughts, *idio-syncratic* thoughts, *idiolectic* thoughts, in them we have the whole or potential of the whole of the human endeavor, the plight of all of human being as far back as it goes, rendered in language, such that it's powerful, language's mode, and the resultant unusual style which will be resultant and unusual and unique to whom-soever employs it, and in turn this *violence*, which can be a *narrative violence*, a *storied violence*, just as much as it can be a *syntactic* one, and resultingly the words will have their force, and they will push back against the comfortable middle as it's been established in the name of so much religious prattling and so much judgmental bog water and horseshit that's made exactly nobody happy sustainably and has allowed a class of artless dip-shits to strangle the gaping maws of all of us staring upward in starved disgust.

I can think of few more delusional statements than "most people are honest".

Finally, I like Deleuze most because of his devotion to pieces of culture, to solidifying his ideas by way of writers, and philosophers, and films, and artists, as this is what I've tried to do when I've sat down and tried to figure something out. I don't know whether art or writing should even concern itself with something like saving the world, or redeeming it, or saving mankind. I don't like or approve of the push for empathy as the reason for serious engagement with this stuff. The serious engagement is what I'm interested in, and the manner it takes, because that's what I found when I picked up these works, when I went to these shows, when I listened to this music.

Submit your science photographs and media files to the Wiki Science Competition!   ✕

Main page
Welcome
Community portal
Village pump
Help center

Language select

English ⌄

Participate

Upload file
Recent changes
Latest files
Random file
Contact us

Tools

What links here
Related changes
Special pages
Permanent link
Page information
Concept URI
Cite this page
Nominate for deletion

Print/export

Download as PDF
Printable version

File:2020-01-16 Curling at the 2020 Winter Youth Olympics – Mixed Team – Gold Medal Game (Martin Rulsch) 113.jpg

From Wikimedia Commons, the free media repository

File   File history   File usage on Commons   File usage on other wikis   Metadata

I don't remember when it was, but sometime back I came across a picture of Peter
Brötzmann, a jazz saxophone and clari-
net and probably several other instrument
performer from Germany, whose heyday I
guess you could say was the 1970s, though
he's still at it today. When I first saw
the picture I had no idea who it was, but
I noticed that his mustache seemed to grow
in the same color as my mustache, and this
comforted me because I've always felt my
mustache was too youthful-looking, faint
as it is, and as a result I'd always cut
my beard and mustache before they got too
long. I looked up more pictures of him,
and saved some for the reason of feeling
less shitty about my facial hair. He also
kind of looked like me, and he was German, and I'm German, so it seemed like
I'd found a person on whom I could model
my look, or whatever. In the process of
looking at images of him I got a sense of
his biography, and then I started listening to his music, and although my knowledge of jazz is relatively minimal, especially the more experimental stuff, I
grew quite fond of his approach, and I've
continued to listen to his stuff, and watch
performances, frequently. There's a video
where he's performing with his quartet,
an improvisation, from 1974 — technically
it's broken into three separate videos,
running a bit over twenty minutes when
played all the way through. Just the first
one is enough, though, at least for me.

6:53 / 8:15

Peter Brötzmann Quartet - improvisation (1974/10/17) (1/3)

445 views

971 DISLIKE SHARE SAVE ...

All From your search Double bass Per

Andrei Ionescu
2.8K subscribers

SUBSCRIBE

Peter Brötzmann Quartet -
improvisation (1974/10/17)...
Andrei Ionescu
9.7K views • 12 years ago

8:16

TVP
KULTURA

It is unfortunately true that you hold the knowledge of the thing you're most going to want to get done within you, and although guidance about history, and craft, and permission can come from classrooms, or even a book like this, the process of developing your work is one of looking inward, and learning to listen to your instincts in the same manner as you might if you were tossed into an ocean and asked to float for a day or more while rescuers came to help. Say before that you'd taken a class where you were given all sorts of ideas about what to do, ways to occupy your time, thoughts to think as you floated there, and techniques for moving your arms and legs that made sense and were based on history, and craft. Snippets of these might prove helpful, but when you're out there you are going to be yourself, and you are going to rely on things, and call upon things within yourself that will make your survival entirely your own. The best things you can give a writer are permission, time, and encouragement in the endeavor they seem to be embarking upon most honestly with their own gut.

I remember sitting in a college class-
room and talking to students about the
nature of language, and pointing at the
table, there, in front of me, and saying "there's nothing in a table that begs
for it to be called a table; nothing that
calls out for the letters t-a-b-l-e in
the thing itself." I think maybe we were
talking about deconstruction, but I can't
be sure. I said more, and one student
repeated "tableness," I remember. I'm
not particularly good at teaching, and
moments like this can really highlight
that. I'm much better at being a moron.

In my body there might be lumps, or sort of dumb little iterations of being, flesh recreated, whatever it is people get in their bodies. I get skin tags, or lumps in my stomach when I worry, which is most of the time. The pancreas is tiny. I don't know where mine is. I don't know what mine is doing in there, anymore. I don't know if I would die. I remember walking home and getting a lift from someone, someone a friend knew, and then getting dropped off closer, and it feeling like it would take forever to get home. The Minnesota Multiphasic Personality Inventory is an autobiography generator, an abstract generator for where your faults lie, and nobody I've ever known who has taken it took it seriously, which is like art. Someone enters into a project in seriousness, and the project won't simply resolve itself and be done in seconds, and so we're stuck there, over these pages, marking things off, and vison gets cloudy, and we don't know whether we're marking the right marks in the right places to indicate what we mean, and so maybe for forty questions we're talking about nothing, or marking things wrong, and then we get bored and decide to fuck with it. And we never hear of it again. I've never felt the worry in my throat, only my gut, my bulbous gut.

The degree to which anything I do could be
said to involve work is stretching things.

I don't like the notion that I'd ever be taken for someone who simply sat around trying to read everything there was in the world. I'm not certain what I mean by this but it's important. I don't necessarily believe that the path to someone becoming a great writer, or even a decent one, is to be mired in texts all the time. This can be the case for many writers, but to my mind there are more important things that happen throughout the day than reading that a writer will pull from. The problem is figuring out these various doses, so that you are a person within this world, not some ancient one. Mario Levrero said once "it's a mistake to expect literature to come only from literary sources."

We have to think about this as every other person thinks about every other thing
within the world. If there are advancements, then we should seek to meet the
world as of those advancements, and oper-
ate from our perception of what is there.
The trouble is when we're beginning to
write we often look to those we view as
authority figures on the subject, and then
we aspire to enact whatever it is they
tell us to do. The trouble there is that
these writers, whoever they are, giving
this advice, aren't in turn acknowledging every circumstance that led to every
single thing they'd ever made, treated
singularly — to pull again from Stein's
ideas. We're much better served if we immerse ourselves into the things that make
our lives whatever they seem to singularly be, to treat language in the way
we tend to treat language, to treat our
projects the way we tend to treat our
projects. Jean Cocteau, whose projects
could not be more disparate and ambling,
said "Listen carefully to first criticisms
made of your work. Note just what it is
about your work that critics don't like
- then cultivate it. That's the only part
of your work that's individual and worth
keeping." This is what I'm advocating, an
awareness of language that's singular, an
approach to writing that may well have
precedent but is the approach that feels
most engaging and compelling for *you*.

It is in my own nature to gravitate toward the poles of emotional distress. This is the first time I've written utilizing an autocorrect suggestion, or not an autocorrect suggestion per se, but a suggestion in that little bar above the keyboard on the iPhone I'm using to type this with. When I was a kid I was emotional. In my marriage I've been the more emotional one. Or more given to letting my emotions overwhelm a situation. I can get really pathetic this way. I don't have a story about it and I don't know whether I even need to have a story about it — can a novel be something other than a story? It seems like it ought to be? I don't know what Robert Musil would say about this because I still haven't read Robert Musil, although I want to. And what is this? We buy a book we know we want to read — or is it that we want to have read it, I can't be sure — and then it lingers there, and not only does it linger there but the thought of picking it up and reading it makes us uncomfortable? Harold Bloom was at least largely full of shit.

Somebody somewhere said that your secrets can be useful things that remind you of who you are. Somebody else said they're no fun. Don DeLillo I think said the former. He's a writer I've read and sometimes loved and sometimes been dulled by. Often I'm dulled. I'm a dullard. I am dull. I dull. In my life I'm always dulling things and being dulled by things. I was never a sharp pencil. Never a Ticonderoga pencil sharpened. Never witty. Never ready. Always slowly mumbling my way over to the bathroom where we'd been playing billiards but I don't drink. Maybe a soda water. My friend might be there or might work there. Eau Claire is a place. I never really made friends. I tagged along and had these half relationships. Now I'm older and there isn't much to say. I think frequently of horrible stuff, and sometimes imagine talking to a therapist about it, but I've talked to therapists, and I don't think I want to talk to any therapist again. Even the people advocating therapy don't seem to advocate therapy anymore. It's just kind of, well, sure, give it a try, I'm a complete mess but sure, give it a try. So I burden the wall, or the car, or my wife, or the rabbit, or the chickens, and it doesn't make me proud, and I don't feel good about it, but who has seventy-five dollars for an hour of conversation. Not me.

I remember reading somewhere this description of Kurt Cobain's stomach problems. That most of the time he was in incredible pain. And that the use of heroin was possibly one of the first things he'd experienced that rectified this. I don't actually recall reading anywhere anybody really confirming he'd even done heroin. Maybe he had with Dylan Carlson. I'm not sure anymore. The starkness of those two extremes, though. The extreme pain that debilitates somebody. The extreme relief of opium. I hate it.

The world is an anxious, rotting thing, and we are here for almost no time, and in the grand scheme of things the human body is this dumb object of intense focus until we're dead, and in accordance with this if we're going to do something we might as well do it all the way. People like to act like this means drink yourself dumb. People like to act like this means be an asshole for ten years. People like to act like this means don't parent, cannibalize your life for the work, devote yourself solely to this thing. This, dumbly, ignores the incredible amount of time in a day. So while you sun yourself on these thoughts of rejecting the whole of living, you're whittling down your sense of things to next to nothing, so you're only able to barely put out a handful of projects in your entire living. The number doesn't matter.

I gave into these things for a long time, and all it ever got me was frantic whenever I found a writer whose work sounded compelling to me. I'd check if they had kids, because I had kids. I checked if they drank, because I'm in recovery. I'd check if they were married, as I was married. All this ever got me were Wikipedia pages, and basically zero art with which I could commune. It hit me more recently, so hopefully I can save you some time: the only thing that I need to share with another writer to make the connection sustainable and nourishing, is writing itself. This hit me when I was trying to find out whether Nathaniel Hawthorne and Herman Melville shared a sort of intimacy that interested me. I was frantic, having looked at their lives, their wives, their children, their stories. I thought I needed to share things with these people and so I was scrolling their Wikipedia pages when suddenly it hit me: the thing that these people devoted their lives to, that compelled them, that gave them pause, that made them look twice, was *writing*. *They were writers, who concerned themselves with writing, and thusly they were mine.* It hit me again when I was reading about Oliver Sacks, a writer and physician my father was interested in. There it was less clear, here was a physician of the highest order, an intellectual whose capacity of genius and understanding leapt over me in every single aspect. But he wrote books. He sat down, and tried to write books. He struggled with them, and got angry with them, and fought his way through their drafting. He worked with sentences, and language, to accomplish something, and this hit me like a long drink of water after walking through an arid plain. They're writers, and that alone can sustain me infinitely.

Search media

🔍 paul metcalf

Images Audio Video Other Media Categories and Pages

License ⌄   File Type ⌄   Image size ⌄   Community Assessments ⌄   Sort by: Relevance ⌄

You are working, in language, to lay bare not only the human experience, but the prism of possible human experiences accessible in any tiny fragment of thought, glint of language, or amassment of sentence-making. Your approach should welcome in the ugly tendencies people have when they get to going about their days. The woman walking into the gas station muttering some half-forgotten Catholic phrasing as she decides whether she'll return to her father's home after facing dire ignominy in the collapse of her career-making artwork in the city. Pay attention to her language, rather than this scene, as what a dull fucking thing a scene would be in the face of all this presence. Mix the mumbled script with the tatters of her long coat and the dumb grunts of the horny fat fuck lording over the cash register. This is the whorl of material that deserves your focus, the actual lingual living of it and not the sketch of some dramatic thing for its dull empty purposing. At the root of every single thing we humans find ourselves encountering is that linguistic stitch, and that is the thing deserving of the writer's attention, and in your sentence-making you are extrapolating the thing outward as much as you feasibly can until your words billow too, and the thing can be made to look like the strange archival fragments of Susan Howe rather than the bland figurements of another scene of apparent import when the words give you the import a thing's got long before the moon glints on the broken glass on the floor.

I remember one night when we thought my adopted brother had run away. I don't remember how old he was. I remember how almost immediately the house we lived in felt kind of foreign, and strange, like everything was suddenly rendered very curious and I was walking through a novel by Horace Walpole. I had no idea who Horace Walpole was back then, of course, but if I'd stopped myself and given myself a brief description of his works I think I'd agree with myself. I remember looking through the basement, suddenly confident even though our basement used to frighten me. I remember looking around our neighborhood and it was night and suddenly it felt kind of exhilarating, which seemed wrong, but I gave myself over to this feeling which surely would've vanished the moment it transpired too long, and we suddenly had to seriously worry he'd run far enough away to not be found, or somebody had kidnapped him and then we'd truly have to worry. We had these bushes by the garage and some of them you could sort of walk into, though they weren't designed for this and thus you'd have to push your way in, and I think my brother was sitting within one of those and sort of laughing, and then I remember someone's shirt being white or vanilla and the situation being swept out of my hands, and then I was back to whatever my life consisted of that day before this minor tragedy. I thought a lot about leaving and always did when I was younger, getting away somewhere. Of course these considerations kind of ran up against real difficulty when I got

type 1 diabetes, and thereafter my fantasies
also involved ways in which I'd rob pharma-
cies to be able to get insulin. So I never
ran away, I just wrote about it in a novel.

The problem I had with the Joker film was it seemed a bit unwieldy, in the worst possible sense of that word. I also don't think the mark of a good actor is their ability to starve themselves and gesture miserably. I'm more impressed with a fat actor who can nevertheless instill something. I think it was stupid when Martin Scorsese and Francis Ford Coppola made their gripes about comic book movies, but I also think we are now at a surplus of this material, and it doesn't interest me much anymore. I tried recently to get into Star Wars again, or I guess to say I try isn't accurate because some of it was natural. On the one hand, I can watch a video of a bunch of sweaty grown men crying at the release of a new Star Wars trailer and become very excited, and inspired, because they're interested in something to such an extent that it consumes them, and that's a beautiful thing. On the other hand, that actual marrow of these things doesn't interest me. That's the trouble. So instead I dabble. I watch some of this thing, while doing this other thing, while reading this other thing, and somehow in this piling on of things I feel alright, but it's rare anymore for one thing to really hold me in its thrall. It does happen, but it's rare. The reality though is that these things aren't meant to hold you in their thrall, as much as they might want to. So I hear about these writers who read hundreds of books a year, and I think sure, that's alright. I also don't think that's too much of a life, the same way that I don't think the life of a monk is much of a life. Lots of people of course don't feel this way, and I've grown to understand that that's OK too. I don't need to connect in every single way with every single being. I don't need to laugh or cry or dream. I don't need to watch *Eyes Wide Shut* again. Maybe my best years are behind me, but much of them weren't too great. I'm a mild person. I've sinned, sure. I get frustrated. I get guilty. I get scared. I'm like anyone. Maybe a little worse. I'm just a person who has a cellphone, and I'm gonna die.

I once lived in my father's basement when I was twenty-three or so. I lived there before this a bit and after a bit. I'm not proud of it, it just was what it was. I don't like to work. That's part of my problem. I'm scared of it. Plus I'm spoiled, which never helps matters. But once I got in school I started to focus more, and I started walking everywhere, and I started to really try to make this writing thing happen for me. I also lived in an apartment in a carriage house with my mother, but eventually moved back into my father's basement because I think I got to be a bit much for my mother. What else. I don't hold grudges exactly. I don't try to get revenge exactly, I think is what this thing is trying to talk to me about. In the morning at my mother's apartment in the carriage house I would wake up early and walk through the neighborhood, then campus, then up this flight of stairs in the dead of winter. I took a class in weight-lifting because you had to take something like that where I got my degree. Then back down the stairs for a biology class, or no it was geology. Then I think a break when I'd work in the library reading, or writing, or doing some combination of either for homework. Then I found out you could rent a little room with a screen for group work, so I rented one and watched a documentary about Andy Warhol. He went to church a lot more than you'd expect.

I

stole.

The experience or event should not be thought of as peculiar or strange, not really. It is only ever our perception of it that is. Someone going for lunch at Culver's in Salt Lake City isn't necessarily strange — I think their Culver's might be just outside the city, potentially in a suburb, but still — but if someone is entering that situation thinking about the whole of their life and the notion that a Butter Burger might in point of fact help them to transcend their misery and laze in a grease-coated position for two hours while reading a book there then it might be thought of as wonderfully strange and exquisitely peculiar. People are people, after all. And yet, I've gone to weird places. My family and I once visited a ranch in Hawaii where they've filmed *Lost*, and *Jurassic Park*, and *Kong: Skull Island*, and on the surface every aspect of it could've been surreal, or something, but I was there with my children, and my wife, and I was enjoying their presence, and not thinking too much about anything else, and thus everything felt very calm, and warmed over, and the things around us from various films didn't even matter all that much. This has been a realization I've been engaging with lately, and maybe it's the change to my antidepressant, but I don't know: a person can adapt to most any thing, and though there are frightening things, and people are scared of any number of things right now, a person does have control, immense control, of their reaction to their circumstance, and atonement is possible, and movement is possible, and love is possible. I believe I dwelled for a long time in a stew of entire hate, and that's alright, but when I'd see the things I'd love, and I'd try and be the person I thought I'd been, I'd feel such conflict in my stomach, and I'd feel so unsettled, and now even in my greatest moments of fear of losing everything that's presently my life, I know that in my thinking I would still honor those things I've lost, and I would love them, and I would atone.

I spent the end of my teen years and the beginning of my twenties eating pretty ravenously. It wasn't just for pleasure, really, but really working to quiet something that existed down within me and make it so that I could almost feel whatever oils, or fats I'd eaten run over my eyeballs as I watched television or prepared to face the remainder of my days. If I had my way, I would eat as much as I wanted of whatever I wanted for the rest of my life. I don't drink, I don't smoke, I don't use drugs, and I don't fuck around, and thus I guess I'd openly accept the notion of eating that way forever as an alternative to these things, although I'd probably get sick or get sick of it and either die or change something. I don't eat as much now but I still eat too much. I think becoming a father and settling down a bit and giving in to a way of eating I'd sort of prepared myself for back when I had a functioning metabolism, I think that these things congealed into the fat ugly mass of me now, and I don't know if there's a way out at this point as I've never been much for exercise. I like to walk. I don't walk much though. I'm in this stupid limbo of the thirty-two year old failure who's fat now and has a job that doesn't pay so well and I have these little books I've published and this family and this little life I've got and I think whatever previous iterations of the kind of guy I might happen to be would flee from this state, and pursue the evils, and not pursuing these evils I have this appetite, and so it feeds me. Perhaps, fat and fair, I'm

I'm an unfamous Orson Welles, with no ci-
gars, and no opinions, and no money, with no
masterpiece to lay my hulking frame atop.

I saw the film *Dear John* in theaters and I wished there were some kind of creature made of stone that could sit down on my chest and I could die.

And should I even talk like this? This stupid fucking way of talking. This fucking salesman way of talking about the work. Why would I give into this stupid fucking banal impulse here? Is it doing anything for you? Can I just fuck off somewheres else and not talk this way not again never ever again? It is the stupid curse of trying to talk about this kind of thing. You find yourself in a film about a person telling an audience about this horse shit. And you tell them. And they hear what they needed to hear and it wasn't you who said it. How else could a book about trying to write things possibly present itself, enact itself like so? This is the great looming thing over all of our heads as we try and give shape to the life we want as writers of sentences. The unknowingness of Blanchot, staring down at yet another day in which we won't know whether our work will be torched or simply ignored. The frenzy of Stein as she tries to give credence to every minor bit of composing while offering the writer a sense of the holy thing they're doing when they sit down. The swerve of Lutz and Lish as they squeeze from each word its resultant word and push them into things that lap around the sea of wordings people carelessly toss out into the air. The problem is you've made the problem, and the path through it is a sentential path, and your inner sense of the language you've got amassed there from all your living will be your map, and as you begin to put it all down there alongside all your other sentence-making the thing will start to grow, and rise up

in reverie with all the old words of others
long dead, and you'll have done it, line by
line, sentence by sentence, piece by piece.

If the history of the human race's efforts on earth have amounted to anything
they've amounted to this. Pessimism though
is easy, so maybe it's not intentional.
I give people too much trouble. People
aren't so bad. I'm not so great and people aren't so bad. I'm bad with money.

In the morning I wake up and my hands are numb. Today I woke up and my hands were numb and my wife had asked me about something and I put my hands up and looked at them and felt their numbness. A sort of dumb thing. A dumb thing, sure. I get these feelings in my body. I'll feel weird and kind of asleep or whatever. In the cold too. In the heat I feel alright. I think I might thrive when I'm old. I'd like to be old and wealthy and live somewhere warm, and spend my time poking around in the garage with different kinds of guitars. I'd like to live a simple life in that respect. I like to be committed to my life. This is something I never was before. Any sense of longevity and I'd run in the opposite direction. When I met my wife, this one glorious summer, I decided I would commit to this person, and this situation, and that I would stop myself if I ever felt like leaving, because those feelings don't feel accurate. Writers will say you gotta lose your life. Says writers, you gotta lose your wife. Says writers, you gotta drink a lot. Says writers, you gotta be bohemian. Says writers, you gotta live in New York City. Says writers, you gotta be dirt poor. Says writers, you gotta have no degrees. Says writers, you gotta have all degrees. Says writers, you gotta experience life. Says writers, you gotta listen to the right music. Says writers, you gotta be willing to get divorced and pissed on and beaten and shit on and you gotta be a shitty parent. Says writers, you gotta run from it all. Says writers, yota go somewhere without language. Says   you gotta experience life. Says writers, you gotta listen to the right music. Says writers, you gotta be willing to get divorced and pissed on and beaten and shit on and you gotta be a shitty parent. Says writers, you gotta run from it all. Says writers, you gotta go somewhere without language. Says writers, the status quo will fuck you up the ass. Says writers, you gotta wear a suit. Says writers, you gotta get an apartment. Says writers, you gotta have no kids. Says writers, you gotta have nine kids. Says writers, you gotta be a piece of shit. Says writers, you gotta go to Harvard, no two ways about it. Says writers, you gotta care about consecution. Says writers, you gotta find the khora. Says writers, you gotta watch Bergman. Says writers, what's your take on Cassavettes. Says writers, you gotta listen to Cybotron. They might be right about that last one. That and drink your mineral water.

I only have confidence in a reactive sense, where I spend most of my time hating myself, and thinking I'm worthless, but if someone hates me, or asserts my worthlessness, I can become like an angry dog, and I guess that's a kind of self-confidence.

When you're with people you're experiencing something akin to mania, and it's too
much, and there's a hope there will come
some quiet soon enough. When I'm with my
wife I don't worry as much as when I'm
with other people. When I'm with other
people I can't express the things I seem
to be taking in, and it's unpleasant. Once
my wife and I went to a casino, and it
was one of the greatest days of my life.

When I was younger I wrote very badly, and I wrote poems, and they were bad, and the prose was bad, and the entirety of my work was bad, and now I'm old, and it's still there.

Someday, I can't say when, I'm going to die. It seems important to breathe it in, that, and not fight it, because possibly it gives you some perspective. The nice thing is it doesn't matter, nobody's there. Nothing is happening.

This book
would not have been written were
it not for
Garielle Lutz, Gertrude Stein,
Blake Butler, Sean Kilpatrick,
Robert Kloss, John Trefry,
Kelsey Maierhofer,
Ada Maierhofer,
Hollis Maierhofer,
Elisabeth Maierhofer,
Christopher Coe, Brian Evenson,
Diane Williams, Christine Schutt,
and countless other writers,
artists, human beings
I'm presently forgetting.
I thank you all sincerely.

Grant Maierhofer
is an American writer,
he lives with his family in
Moscow, Idaho.

FERAL DOVE

PUBLISHED BY

FERAL DOVE

BOOKS

ISBN 979-8-9856764-9-5

FIRST EDITION

Thank you for being here.

Cover & interior book design by
Evan Femino

www.feraldove.com

Printed in the USA
CPSIA information can be obtained
at www.ICGtesting.com
JSHW060219150624
64775JS00006B/30